THE FEARLESS FLIER'S HANDBOOK

Learning to Beat the Fear of Flying
with the Experts from the Qantas Clinic

DEBBIE SEAMAN

Ten Speed Press
Berkeley, California

A Kirsty Melville Book

Ten Speed Press
P.O. Box 7123
Berkeley, California 94707
www.tenspeed.com

Distributed in Australia by Simon and Schuster Australia, in Canada by Ten Speed Press Canada, in New Zealand by Southern Publishers Group, in South Africa by Real Books, and in the United Kingdom and Europe by Airlift Book Company.

Illustrations by Robert Fischer
Text design by Victor Ichioka
Cover design and illustration by Kathy Warinner

Art credits: Pages 38, 54, 67, 69, 70, 73, 74, 75, and 105: courtesy of the Boeing Company. Page 66: diagram courtesy of Boeing; additional information courtesy of Qantas. Page 92: courtesy of the Australian Bureau of Meteorology. Page 102: courtesy of the National Weather Service. Pages 125 and 140: courtesy of the Federal Aviation Administration. Page 193: Warren Lancaster.

Library of Congress Cataloging-in-Publication Data

Seaman, Debbie.
    The fearless fliers handbook : learning to beat the fear of flying with experts from the Qantas Clinic / Debbie Seaman.
        p.   cm.
    ISBN 1-58008-029-4 (alk. paper)
        1. Fear of flying—Handbooks, manuals, etc.   2. Air travel—Psychological aspects—Handbooks, manuals, etc.
    RC1090.S37   1998
    616.85'225—DC21   98-27263
                                                              CIP

First printing, 1998

Printed in the United States of America

4 5 6 7 8 9 10 — 07 06 05 04 03

To Warren Lancaster,
the world's best husband,
for his love and support.

———————

To Glenda Philpott of Fearless Flyers,
for her help with my recovery
and with this book, and especially for
this eminently worthy calling that
changes so many lives for the better.

———————

To my father, Alfred Seaman,
for teaching me that
"we are judged by our actions."

ARE YOU A FEARFUL FLIER?

Give an honest "Yes" or "No" answer to the following questions:

Do you insist on or have you ever insisted on making a long trip in the car to avoid getting on a plane?

Do you get superstitious about your plane reservations, and are you unwilling to change them once they are booked?

Do you start experiencing feelings of dread about flying, even days before you are due at the airport?

Do you get separation anxiety before you leave on a flight, fearful that you're not going to see family and friends again?

Have you ever canceled a reservation or not shown up at the airport because you were afraid to take a flight?

Do you become afraid even when you drop off family members or friends at the airport?

Do you worry about the competence of your pilot or the jet maintenance staff?

Does the safety briefing by the flight attendants or in a film get you imagining worst-case scenarios?

Do you have a strong urge to get off the plane once the doors are closed, because you think your flight is doomed?

Have you ever had a panic attack at any stage of a flight, i.e., broken out in a sweat, had heart palpitations, experienced numbness in your fingers and hands, had the shakes, or had difficulty breathing?

Do you ever make sure you have plenty of alcohol under your belt before and during a flight just to ease your fears? Or take tranquilizers before getting on a plane?

Do you think your plane is too big to get off the ground? Do you become nervous during take-off, afraid that the plane is simply going to drop out of the sky?

Are you upset by noises the plane makes or changes in engine velocity?

Are you afraid to look out a plane window?

Do you stiffen in fright every time the plane hits a patch of turbulence, worried that it's going to be knocked out of the sky?

Do you find yourself having negative fantasies about what's going to happen to the plane and how you are going to feel as it's going down?

In bad weather or fog, do you worry that the pilot will get lost or crash into another plane?

Are you nervous as the plane is flying over water?

When the plane starts its descent, do you start worrying that it will crash-land or miss the runway?

During a flight, do you ever swear to yourself that you'll never get on another plane in your life, if you can only get to your destination safely?

If you answered "Yes" to three or more of these questions, you need to read this book!

CONTENTS

FRIGHTENED OF FLYING?
YOU'RE NOT ALONE

*When you have this kind of fear of something,
it's very isolating.*

—Karen Tomlinson
Fearless Flyers class of November 1993

If you, like me, have suffered from fear of flying, you're in good company. Fear of flying affects as many as one in five people to some degree. For some, the fear is so paralyzing that they have never boarded a plane. Flying has always been a necessary evil for others: They'll do it because they have to, but it's a torturous trip. Many others, like myself, never used to be bothered by flying and considered it part of the excitement of travel before a frightening incident eroded their confidence in air travel and gave birth to a debilitating phobia.

So we avoid flying and miss out on promotions and business opportunities as well as a lot of fun visiting new places.

Or we fly—dreading it, then "white-knuckling" it—and get off the plane at our destinations feeling as though we've taken years off our lives.

Or we wake up and get help.

An American freelance journalist married to an Australian and living in Sydney, I was fortunate enough to get that help from Fearless Flyers, an eight-session course run by members of the Australian Women Pilots Association at the Sydney airport—using the facilities of Qantas as well as volunteer speakers from the airline—which can be considered a model program for people everywhere who suffer from fear of flying. When it was founded in Australia in 1979, Fearless Flyers adopted the same format and methods used by the renowned Fear of Flying Clinic in San Mateo, California. The Australian clinic then joined forces with Qantas. Since the airline was started in 1920 to fly passengers to remote areas of Australia, Qantas has had one of the best safety records of any airline worldwide, a status it works hard to maintain.

I enjoyed and profited from the Australian Fearless Flyers course so much that I wanted to pass on the reassuring, healing knowledge and wisdom of the volunteers who teach it. Having failed to get any comfort from the other books on conquering fear of flying, in which it was the authors who explained why flying was safe—I bought several of these before writing this book and tried them out as maintenance tools during flights—I wanted to write a book for fearful fliers who, like me, preferred to get their information straight from the horse's mouth, as it were. I wanted to hear it from the pilots, the mechanics, the air traffic controllers, the flight attendants, and other aviation experts.

You'll be hearing from a variety of voices in this book—experts from all the different realms of aviation.

- Qantas captain Lyn Williams answers some of the questions most frequently asked by fearful fliers, such as, "What happens if all four engines on a 747 fail?"

- Ken Dunkley, Qantas manager of mechanical systems engineering, will tell you not only how a plane stays in the air but also how fastidiously jets are maintained—with a detailed record kept of the maintenance history of each jet part.

- Paul Blanch, Qantas manager of flight engineer training, who takes Fearless Flyers groups for "spins" at the controls of an ultra-realistic flight simulator, explains why the different noises a plane makes should be reassuring instead of unnerving.

- Ken Anderson, Qantas senior check flight engineer, sits with me in the cockpit of a Boeing 747 flight simulator during a flight crew's recurrent training session and explains the often grueling exercises they are put through to practice handling malfunctions and tricky situations.

- Retired Qantas senior flight attendant Marie Williams tells about the stringent training of attendants and how they are tested regularly on safety measures to keep them on their toes.

- Outside Qantas, Steve Symonds of the Australian Bureau of Meteorology explains why we need never fear turbulence and other weather events as long as we have our seat belts fastened.

- Psychologist Dr. Bryan Burke talks about the types of people who suffer from fear of flying and describes ways in which fearful fliers can take back control of their feelings.

- Alan Dukes, an air traffic controller at the Sydney airport, makes it clear that the control tower we see is only the tip of the iceberg as far as air traffic control is concerned and that, from the time a plane leaves its gate to the moment it arrives at the destination gate, somebody is watching to make sure it doesn't get close to another plane.

- Ron Morgan, director of air traffic control for the Federal Aviation Administration (FAA) in the United States, tells why it is as safe to fly into the New York area, where there are several airports and lots more air traffic, as it is to fly into less congested Sydney.

The Fearless Flier's Handbook is based on interviews with these experts and several graduates of the course, a couple of whom have gone on to take flying lessons. Even if you don't think you'll ever fly a plane, you will recognize yourself in parts of their stories and realize that you, too, can learn to fly comfortably.

If fear of flying is wreaking havoc with your quality of life and you have taken the vital first step of admitting that you can't manage it by yourself, this handbook will become a course in itself and help you recover. The information herein pertains not to one airline or one country but to aviation worldwide.

The Fearless Flier's Handbook is also meant for people like me, who have graduated from a course but may need a "refresher" because they have had a lengthy gap between trips.

The day after I took my Fearless Flyers graduation flight on a Boeing 747 from Sydney to Melbourne and back (one hour each way), I boarded a sixteen-seater twin-engine jet and traveled with no problems from Sydney to Broken Hill, a historic mining town in the Australian Outback where I was to do a feature for an American travel magazine. I even asked to sit in on the landing and felt a rush of excitement as the plane seemed to hang suspended above the runway before swooping down to land. Four months later, I made a round-the-world trip in three weeks, with barely a heightened pulse. The purpose of these flights was either for work, to pursue the traveling I so loved, or to visit my family in New York, and the difference in my emotional state, compared to how I once had been, was dramatic. I could finally fly calmly rather than in terror.

Then, even though I had been told that I needed to keep flying regularly to maintain my recovery, I went seven months without flying. I experienced a bout of nerves during my next air trip between Sydney and the States to take my twin boys to see my family. Especially unnerving was the climb out of Los Angeles to Sydney, more gradual than I had ever experienced. Even though I should have known that the low altitude at which the plane was climbing was probably directed by air traffic control, I was seized with panic, thinking that the 747 just could not climb and would belly-flop in the Pacific. Rather than play back the information I had learned in the course or do some deep breathing, I allowed my own "horror movies" to take over.

The TWA Flight 800 disaster only a couple of months later, on July 17, 1996—when a 747 exploded in a fireball just after taking off from New York's JFK Airport, killing all 230 people aboard—threatened to negate any progress I'd made. I was back in Sydney at the time and was haunted by the accident and subsequent media reports, sure that I could never get on a plane again.

A few months after TWA Flight 800, after I'd nervously made plane reservations to fly back to New York with my husband and children for Christmas, I picked up the phone and called Glenda Philpott, Fearless Flyers's leader. She generously offered to let me come back and sit in on a class then in progress. After hearing a Q&A session with a Qantas senior captain, I skipped out of that classroom and happily would have hopped on the Wright brothers' first plane, had anyone suggested it.

That was when I decided to write *The Fearless Flier's Handbook*. I knew that I could bring this marvelous course and its teachers to other fearful fliers who could not or would not attend a course. Also, having just acknowledged that my problem might need regular, ongoing treatment to keep it in remission, I realized that, for me and others like me, the book would be a tool at our fingertips to remind us that it was okay to fly.

So read this book before and during your next flight. It should give you a new sense of security on an airplane, as well as a new respect for the aviation industry. I don't want to gloss over the fact that incidents and accidents do happen—no system is perfect, after all—but they are rare, and people in aviation around the world are working to ensure that flying gets even safer. So instead of being alarmed, for example, when a manufacturer recalls a certain model of jet to make adjustments, you should instead feel heartened that potential problems have been averted.

Above all, this book will help you focus on the positive. In fact, a positive attitude is essential to your recovery from fear of flying. You must be willing, first, to work to change your self-sabotaging habits and thoughts and replace them with new, constructive ones, and second, to get help with this.

That kind of motivation is usually brought about when one's old ways become too self-destructive and painful, even tormenting. I'll describe in the next chapter the anguish that drove me to seek help.

MY STORY: STRUGGLING IN THE GRIP OF TERROR

*I become frightened by strange noises in the cabin
and even subtle changes in the whirr of the engines.
When something sounds different, I go on high
alert. My stomach tightens, and my pulse speeds up.
I immediately look around the cabin to see if other
passengers are concerned, and I focus on the flight
attendants to judge their reactions. Invariably
everyone else is oblivious to the sounds that concern
me, and I wonder if I'm the only one that knows.*

—Brian Kinahan, fearful flier
Chapel Hill, North Carolina

Our flight was halfway between New York and Washington, D.C., when we felt the plane drop out of the sky. The aircraft lost altitude so suddenly and dramatically that the passengers gave a collective gasp. Gripped with gut-wrenching terror, my knuckles white and my face contorted in horror, I was convinced not only that I was about to die violently but that, for several more minutes, I would continue to be exquisitely conscious of this inevitability until our plane plummeted to the earth in a ball of fire.

Of course, the plane leveled off quickly. The pilot, in the same cozy drawl he'd used to give us the weather report, came on the PA system to inform us that he'd had to avoid a small aircraft. Some smaller private airplanes are not required to be under air traffic control surveillance; obviously this one wasn't able to steer clear of other aircraft adequately on its own.

This incident, which took place in mid-1984, has likely been forgotten by most of the other people on that plane. For me, however, it was the moment when flying began to inspire dread instead of excitement. With each consecutive flight—and I've always been a frequent traveler—the fear seemed to feed upon itself until, a couple of years later, it had blossomed into a bona fide phobia.

When I boarded an aircraft, all I had to do was look at the nose of the plane, imagining it thousands of feet above the earth, and I felt the first ripple of panic. The takeoffs were the worst. As the jet gathered speed and lumbered heavily skyward, I was sure that the plane would simply lose momentum and crash. During those moments, I felt that my getting on the plane was a mistake I'd never be able to right because we wouldn't make it to our cruising altitude, let alone our destination, alive. Although I'd been told a hundred times that I was safer in the air than on the road, I was sure that I would lose this particular lottery. How many times, after all, had I read about jet crashes with horror and fascination and imagined the plight of the passengers during those last seconds? Even as the plane taxied down the runway and everything seemed safe, I'd remind myself that every doomed flight had begun just as innocuously. And when the talking head in the safety film cheerfully said, "In the event of a water landing"—what a euphemism, I thought!—I'd imagine the jet crashing and sinking in distant shark-infested waters.

As the plane ascended, I'd go into a downward spiral. I would break out in a sweat, my chest would tighten, and even planting my feet firmly on the floor would fail to ground me. I felt emotionally flayed. I had control neither over the feelings I was host to—terror, discomfort, vulnerability, and downright dislike and distaste—nor over their snowballing. Coupled with this fear was an intense longing not to be present, not to be in my own skin. I swore that if I ever reached terra firma, I'd never leave it again.

The discomfort was exacerbated by the slightest changes in sounds from the engine or any other part of the plane. "What's that?" I'd gasp to my husband, my fingers digging into his arm, as I heard a high, whining sound in the bowels of the jet. ("Nothing out of the ordinary," he'd reply, looking at me as if I were mad.) "Why is the plane doing that?" I'd demand of a bemused attendant, who explained that the minor fits and starts I felt during takeoff were merely caused by the wind. Even the loud signal that summoned the attendants was enough to make me nearly jump out of my seat, convinced every time that it was an alarm signaling an impending loss of cabin pressure.

Once the aircraft had reached its cruising altitude, my emotions were manageable as long as we didn't hit any major turbulence. Landings were almost tolerable because I figured we were close enough to the ground that the plane ought to be able to get down safely. But on night flights, as I tried to sleep, the roar of the engines would remind me that I was in a mere capsule blasting through a vast, black void—an unnatural state for humans if ever there was one—and I'd simply capsize emotionally.

Once when I was living and working as a freelance journalist in Paris, I managed to go a whole year without flying. I discovered the high-speed TGV and happily crisscrossed Europe by train. But then I was compelled to fly. I got the opportunity for a paid business trip from Paris to Singapore and then decided to pay my own way to Australia from there, since I'd always wanted to visit that country. As it turned out, I looked up the man I'd met in Paris more than a year before and fell madly in love, so I went back to see him four months later. (He was to become my husband!) Right after that second trip to Australia, I flew from Paris to New York to surprise my father on his eightieth birthday.

Out of all those trips and many to come, I can recall only one fearless flight. That was when I'd gotten food poisoning at a hotel at Newark Airport just prior to departure and was so deathly ill all the way across the Atlantic that I couldn't have cared less if the plane crashed.

Later, married and living in Sydney, Australia, I was writing an increasing number of travel articles at different destinations within Australia and making marathon trips from that island continent to New York. But after a while I couldn't even turn to my husband anymore. He adores flying, especially the takeoff, and I was jealous that he could enjoy something I so hated. Once when we were en route to New York from Sydney with our infant twin boys and I whimpered that I couldn't abide this terror any longer, he snapped, "Well, do something about it!"

That was a radical idea! Yet I'd compared notes with enough fellow fearful fliers to know that my misery had company, and I'd heard of the existence of many fear-of-flying clinics. I even had met someone who had refused to get on a plane for twelve years but was now happily hopping continents for his job since taking a fear-of-flying course.

In January of 1995, soon after my husband had suggested I get help, I contacted the course my friend had recommended: Fearless Flyers, Inc., a nonprofit organization run by a small group of members of the Australian Women Pilots Association and sponsored by Qantas at that airline's headquarters at the Sydney airport. This clinic met for three hours every Tuesday night for eight weeks, offering everything from instruction in relaxation techniques to talks by Qantas captains and visits to air traffic control and jet maintenance facilities. The only catch was that the fee included a round-trip from Sydney to Melbourne at the end of the course, and that made my blood run cold. My first thought was that the flight would surely crash, with twenty fearful fliers aboard, gingerly testing their wings. "Some headline that will make," the journalist in me thought darkly.

The bottom line, however, was that flying was an inescapable fact of life for me. I resolved that I wanted to stop huddling in my seat during takeoffs, thinking, "I can never again in my life go through this terror."

I wanted to get well.

WHAT FEARLESS FLYERS
IS ALL ABOUT

At long last there was an opportunity to overcome my fear. . . . I approached the course with a positive feeling.

—Donald Evans
first Fearless Flyers student, October 1979

As I and nineteen fellow fearful fliers walked into a large, brightly lit room at the Qantas Jet Base one night in February 1995, we joined a long line of souls who had sought succor before us.

It started with the pharmacist in his late forties who had caught the travel bug and was determined to beat the crippling fear of flying that threatened to confine him to cars and cruise ships for the remainder of his life; the young woman who wanted to be able to fly from Australia to America to wed her fiancé; and the businessman who longed to visit his son in London.

When these and six other equally terrified people filed into the very first Fearless Flyers class in October 1979, Glenda Philpott and her colleagues were ready. By the time the course was over, these students had been immersed in the world of aviation in a way few "civilians" have the opportunity to be. They boarded a Qantas "graduation flight" from Sydney to Melbourne and began their recovery in earnest.

Fearless Flyers co-founder Glenda Philpott is still in touch with several members of that first class, just as she continues to get phone calls, as well as postcards from exotic destinations, from many of the hundreds of people she has helped fly comfortably over the years. We are grateful to all the people from the course, from the friendly support staff who fed us homemade sandwiches and cakes at the dinner breaks to the Qantas employees who taught us what really went on behind the "wings," as it were. But it is Philpott whom we continue to inform of our successes and look to for reassurance in the work remaining long after the course is done.

How the Course Began

All the best fear-of-flying courses surely have Glenda Philpott's counterparts, but to her students she is unique. A tall, solid woman nicknamed the "Gentle Giant" by the man who ran the flying club where she got her instructor's rating, Philpott has a passion for flying that her collection of colorful airplane earrings only hints at. "Learning to fly is a bit like a drug addiction—once you start, you want to keep going and be involved more and more," she tells me. "Because I enjoy flying so much, I like to share that love with people who are afraid of flying."

Philpott taught high school geography and economics before, at thirty-something, she took a break from teaching to learn to fly at Hoxton Park, an airfield to the west of Sydney. Before long, she had bought a single-engine red-and-white Beechcraft Muscateer from the flying school. By 1976, she had replaced her first plane with a twin-engine Piper Aztec and had attained a commercial license to pilot charter flights, followed with an instructor's rating in 1977.

Philpott had just adopted an infant daughter with her husband, Albert, and was pregnant with another when her other "baby"— Fearless Flyers—was born. It began in August 1978 at a conference for the 99s, the International Organization of Women Pilots, in Australia. Here, Philpott, along with colleagues Aminta Hennessy and Nancy Wells, met up with Fran Grant, a member of the San Francisco 99s. Grant, with Jeanne McElhatton, had cofounded the Fear of Flying Clinic at San Francisco International Airport in California, in 1976, with the support of United Airlines. Grant offered to help her Australian colleagues duplicate the program.

The Australian women, all members of the Australian Women Pilots Association, were excited by the idea and resolved that any proceeds from the course would be put toward scholarships for female pilots. Qantas agreed to provide the clinic with facilities and aviation experts and consented to carry most of the cost of the tickets for the graduation flights. The Australian clinic, which later took on the name Fearless Flyers, signed up its first participants in late 1979.

Philpott credits her colleagues Hennessy and Wells with getting the Australian course off the ground. But she, who with Marion Edwards flew to San Mateo to learn to teach the clinic, was involved in the Australian course from the first night. Several years later, Hennessy stepped down as leader of the course and Philpott took over. Running the Fearless Flyers program out of her home is just one of Philpott's many callings—she has her real estate broker's license and teaches the subject at a local college—but it is her most gratifying. "We're taking people by the hand and showing them there's nothing to fear," she says.

The Structure of the Course

I had to be taken by the hand at first but was soon put at ease by Philpott and the other volunteers, some themselves graduates of the course. I remember how comforting it was to hear the testimonies of former fearful fliers on the first night, including people who had gone on to fly themselves. Still I reflected that I would be quite happy, thank you very much, with simply becoming a placid passenger.

I found it reassuring that one in five people suffers from the fear of flying. The bad news was that there was no "magic pill" to cure it and that, paradoxically, we were going to have to work hard at relaxation. A positive attitude was another necessity. "If your boss is paying and you don't want to be here, you won't get better," Philpott warned.

We classmates got to know one another, first pairing off, then talking in small groups, then finally introducing ourselves in a large circle. A couple of people were worse off than me—two had never seen the interior of a plane—but I could identify with everyone's story. Eerily, we all shared the conviction when boarding a plane that our flight would be that odd statistic that wouldn't make it. Some of us even had the same dream of watching a huge jet crash before our eyes.

We soon took the first steps in overcoming those fears. Dr. Bryan Burke, a psychologist at the University of New South Wales in Sydney, taught us relaxation exercises: a combination of deep, slow breathing and the tensing and releasing of different muscle groups. The lesson, repeated in the following weeks, was that we had the power to change the way we were feeling.

More fun, however, was the exposure we received to every aspect of aviation. We ascended the Sydney airport air traffic control tower— hardly the hotbed of stress I'd expected—and watched, mesmerized, as jets took off and landed on a clear night. We went on a "jet crawl," an exploration inside, around, and under a 747 docked in a Qantas hangar, a session designed for desensitization. Two people in the class wept on board the plane but said later that the cry had been cathartic.

Another night, we toured the flight crew training center, complete with swimming pool, where crew members were taught to evacuate a plane virtually blindfolded. Although we were told that a plane can land on water and shown how the evacuation chutes double as life rafts, this was not a comfortable scenario to imagine, so it was good to get this segment over with early on. Yet, beyond reassuring us of our chances of survival in the unlikely case of an accident, it changed our perception of flight attendants from that of waitresses and waiters to highly trained and stringently tested safety officers.

The Qantas staff members who came to talk with us did not flinch when fielding questions about sensitive subjects such as malfunctions and accidents, but for obvious reasons, the emphasis was on safety. We were taught, for example, that pilots are prepared for any eventuality. They regularly visit the airline's flight simulators to practice dealing with malfunctions such as an engine failure. During the actual takeoff, we were told, pilots always assume that an engine is going to fail (though they rarely do) and are always ready to take appropriate action.

A video on jet maintenance—as well as a tour of the jet maintenance center—showed us how these giant machines are gone over with the finest of fine-tooth combs, and another film demonstrated the dependability of a 747 by showing that it can take off even after its tail end is dragged along the runway while its front end is airborne. That film came to mind in the most comforting manner later on, when I was going through some of the first takeoffs of my recovery.

Of course, they didn't forget weather and turbulence! We learned to eradicate the term "air pocket" from our vocabularies and think of the air as a fluid in motion, like the sea. We discovered that the only harm that could come to us from turbulence was injury as a result of unfastened seat belts. We were educated about "wind shear" and how pilots are trained to handle it.

Our instruction went on to cover a variety of other aspects of aviation, from aerodynamics to engine noises. No single part of the course, however, did as much to make me feel better about flying as did a whirl in one of Qantas's AUS $22 million (US $14.3 million) flight simulators. So realistic are the cockpits of these machines and their sounds and movements that I panicked after I'd impetuously volunteered to "fly" the 747 simulator.

Fear turned to awe as, under the tutelage of Qantas manager for flight engineer training Paul Blanch, I got this "jumbo jet" into the air from the Hong Kong airport and kept it up, marveling at the sensitivity of the instruments in the cockpit as I banked to turn to the left. I'm still not sure why this ride seemed so reassuring, aside from the fact that it demonstrated the handiness of even such a huge machine. Perhaps it was because those of us who worried about not being in control felt more secure having experienced the pilot's role ourselves. All students got the opportunity to "fly" the simulator if they wanted to.

The Graduation Flight

The graduation flight at the end of the course allowed us to experience the "real thing" with the support of classmates, the Fearless Flyers support staff, and some of our teachers. Looking back on that flight, I can see that the same old triggers set me off: the movements of the climb, the engine sounds, the bumps of turbulence. The crucial difference this time was that the fear lasted only until my mind fed what I'd learned in the course back to me. When the jet changed course and tilted, for example, I was able to think of it as a cradle being rocked, an analogy Philpott had taught us. When the power was cut back as we were still climbing, I knew we no longer needed the same level of acceleration and did not conclude that we were about to pitch into the sea below. As we hit the inevitable turbulence, my newfound awareness of its harmlessness quelled the first stabs of panic. And I had to admit that when I compared this relatively mild anxiety to the terror that used to grip me in the air, I knew I was getting better.

For Glenda Philpott, a graduation flight is perhaps even more trying than for the students. Like a mother hen, she goes around making sure her pupils are comfortable, confident, and most important, doing their relaxation exercises. She sits and talks patiently with the less confident and holds their hands if necessary. "On that day, I'm hoping each person is going to get over their fear or make great progress," she explains. "The biggest disappointment is somebody who doesn't show up on the day of the flight."

Fortunately, success stories are in the overwhelming majority among Fearless Flyers, and you'll be reading six of them in the pages to come, tucked between the chapters that will familiarize you with the world of aviation. The first tale of graduates getting their wings is that of Kathryn Bendall, in the next chapter. You will relate to her fear and be inspired by her recovery!

FORCED TO MAKE A CHOICE: KATHRYN BENDALL'S STORY

I wonder if the strange hissing sound from over-head is a leak in the fuselage or a short-circuit in the plane's control system. Will we suddenly lose power and begin to drop — no, plummet! — to earth 30,000 feet below? What will it be like nose-diving at high speed with hundreds of people around screaming and throwing up?

Brian Kinahan, fearful flier
Chapel Hill, North Carolina

One day in 1995, Kathryn Bendall got what should have been exhil-arating news. Called in by a supervisor at the large insurance and home loan company she worked for, she was told that she had been chosen to head up an important national marketing project for the company.

A large increase in salary wasn't the only perk the company was offering. The supervisor leaned forward in her chair and, smiling as if she was about to tell Bendall she had won the lottery, informed her that the new post meant that the company would be flying her all over Australia.

Bendall turned the job down flat.

Puzzled to the point of shock, Bendall's bosses misunderstood. They tried again and upped the salary. "That was the crunch," Bendall sighs today, remembering that's when she realized it was finally time to get help for her fear of flying.

For many people, the fear of flying is a signal of past or present dif-ficulties in other areas of their lives. It wasn't until Bendall took the Fearless Flyers course in Sydney that she realized she had been such a case. Now a mother of three and successful executive at forty-six, she pinpoints the onset of her phobia to the illness of her first husband in 1979. When he called her from South Australia, where he had been working for three months, to tell her he had testicular cancer, she left their two toddlers at home with relatives and flew down there to be at his side.

While Bendall had been a support to her husband during her brief stay in South Australia, the flight home marked the beginning of Bendall's emotional demise. "Everything was horrible," Bendall recalls. "I felt so uptight on the plane coming back. I was panic-stricken about everything. I felt I couldn't manage my life anymore—that it was too big for me."

Her husband eventually found out that he had been misdiagnosed, but the marriage broke up two years later. Bendall, meanwhile, had no compelling reason to fly until she remarried and flew to New Zealand on a honeymoon with her new husband in 1986. The panic came back with a vengeance. "I was really, really fearful," she relates. "Physically, there was numbness in my hands and feet as well as a sensation that felt like pins and needles. My mouth was dry, and I felt rigid inside—as if, if I let go, I'd disintegrate."

Fear of the feelings mounting inside her exacerbated the problem, and she worried that people around her would perceive her fear. "I was afraid I'd lose control and stand up and scream and run through the plane," Bendall admits. "I'd watch the attendants' faces to see if they could see how terrified I was."

Not long after she returned from her honeymoon in New Zealand, Bendall found out she was pregnant. She subsequently made a commitment to start trying to conquer anxieties she felt were interfering with her personal development, such as fear of rejection. So in 1989 she went out and got a job selling insurance. And found out she was good at it!

Less than a year later, Bendall was doing such a good job that the insurance company wanted her to fly to Melbourne for a project. She didn't dare refuse, as she felt that all the hard work she'd done would be for naught, but before that flight to Melbourne, she was awake half the night, suffering from stress-induced diarrhea. Even traveling to the airport was nerve-racking, and she felt worse when she got on the plane. "I thought I'd addressed all my fears—of rejection, dealing with people, dealing with life," she says. "Then there I was sitting in business class between two men working with laptops. I thought, 'How can they just sit there calmly when we're all going to die?'"

Everything about flying scared Bendall: "The bumps, the noises, the vibrations—the more I obsessed about it, the more I noticed things. The whole thing didn't make sense: How could this big, heavy thing stay in the air? I had visions of the plane plummeting to earth—that there'd be no second chance. I imagined how I'd feel, what my last thoughts would be as the plane went down." Back came the pins and needles, and Bendall's salivary glands ceased to function when she was offered a drink or a meal.

Once back on solid ground, Bendall vowed never to go through such terror again. She did not have to until 1995, when her father announced that he intended to take the entire family and grandchildren on a dream holiday to a luxury resort on the tropical coast of Queensland, a state in Australia's northeast. Bendall was in a real quandary, not able to stand the thought of being in a plane for two-plus hours but not willing to tell her children they couldn't go. "Also, I didn't want my children to see how frightened I was," she says.

So she went on the trip, clutching the arm of her husband, Ron, through the entire plane ride. Unable to eat or drink, Bendall became so pale that a flight attendant came over to ask her if everything was okay. Of course it wasn't, but talking to that attendant and other attendants helped a bit. "I felt some relief talking to them," she remembers. "I realized that these people flew all the time, and I was struck by how relaxed they were and how ordinary the whole experience seemed to them. I realized that my fear didn't make sense."

Ron Bendall agreed that his wife's fear didn't make sense. His frustration later came to a head when she insisted that the family take a ten-hour trip in the car, with the kids fighting in the back seat, so that she could avoid flying. "You're going to have to do something about this fear of flying," he told her on the way back.

Bendall, at this point a department manager for her company, also knew she couldn't go any farther up the corporate ladder if she couldn't get on a plane. Her career seemed as if it was at a dead end until the company offered her the national marketing job, even increasing its initial salary offer. As fate would have it, while Bendall was mulling over her dilemma, she ran into her old friend Julie Robertson, also at her company, who happened to be one of the women pilots who lend their support during the Fearless Flyers courses. Robertson arranged for Bendall to be enrolled for the next course, which, serendipitously, was to start the following week.

Bendall didn't tell her bosses about her problem but accepted the new job. It was the right decision. "Within a week of finishing the Fearless Flyers course, I started flying—and flying a lot!" she relates. The first few times she brought along the relaxation tapes from the course and listened to them on a portable cassette player while practicing her deep breathing in her seat. Eventually, she knew the exercises so well that she could do them without the instructional tape.

Bendall also worked hard at replacing her negative thoughts with positive ones. "Flying is the way I get to the thing I'm looking forward to," she explains. "I build up in my mind the pleasure that's awaiting." When flying to Melbourne, for example, she learned to visualize the luxury business hotel she stayed in and the Melbourne colleagues she liked to work with. Or she'd flip on the comedy channel on the airline headphones and concentrate on the jokes. "I feel calm in the plane now," she adds. "I feel really, really relaxed and take each sensation as it comes. I'm not frantic anymore."

As a result of her work on the marketing project, Bendall's company promoted her to head up its sponsorship program for the Sydney 2000 Olympics. From there, she landed an exciting job with the Sydney Organizing Committee for the Olympic Games itself.

Other triumphs have been smaller but gratifying nevertheless. Bendall really knew she'd come a long way, for example, when members of her family started noticing that they no longer were able to predict when she was due to fly the next day. "No more going outside looking at the clouds and obsessing about the weather," she laughs. "That's just one of many things that have changed."

VICTIMS NO MORE: THE PSYCHOLOGY OF BEATING THE FEAR OF FLYING

*I'd go to the airport and watch the planes take off,
and I'd relate that to the height off the ground, and
that would spark all these feelings.*

—Wayne Norman
Fearless Flyers class of November 1995

L ike a lot of fearful fliers, I wanted to be able to take a magic pill to
do what all those prescription tranquilizers of yore could not:
eradicate my terror and make me feel comfortable on a plane.
I wanted Glenda the Good Witch to wave her wand and render me an
ace air traveler, or at least someone who didn't cringe every time the
sounds of the plane's engines changed pitch or the plane encountered
some bumpy weather.

How disappointing it was, therefore, to find out there were no
quick fixes and that I was going to have to work hard at this relaxation
business! The bad habits of sabotaging myself with destructive thinking
and running horror movies in my head, featuring worst-case scenarios
in which I starred as victim, were not something I could get over in a
day, or even a week.

The good news is that, by diligently refocusing their thoughts and
practicing certain mental and physical exercises, people can take back
control of their feelings in the air, or in any other stressful situation. "It's
okay to be afraid—it's what you *do* about being afraid that matters,"
stresses Bryan Burke, the counseling psychologist who teaches this
aspect of recovery to fearful fliers. His teachings are as crucial a part of
the Fearless Flyers course as the education about aviation safety and in
fact are introduced the first night of the course, before participants learn
anything about planes. Because it is impossible to feel afraid if mentally
and physically relaxed, we not only went through Burke's relaxation
exercises at various times throughout the course but were instructed to
practice them at home twice a day. Those of us who did this rigorously,
we were told, would enjoy a speedier and more enduring recovery than
those who didn't.

Here, Burke shares his observations about fearful fliers and
describes the steps they need to take to give themselves the best shot at

recovery. For those who want to make their own relaxation tapes, a transcript of one of Burke's can be found in the back of the book on page 185.

THE PSYCHOLOGIST'S PERSPECTIVE BY DR. BRYAN BURKE

My fundamental goal in the Fearless Flyers course is to help people realize that they have no control over the aircraft or the pilot—a situation I'm very thankful for because the last thing I want up there is a bloody amateur! What they do have a lot of control over is themselves, how they think, and, ultimately, how they feel.

Most people who develop a fear of flying are what we might call worriers. They are very cautious people who, generally speaking, worry about a lot of things besides flying. Part of the reason they worry is that they believe they don't have any influence or control over what happens in the air or elsewhere. In other words, they see themselves as helpless victims.

The basic proposition we work with in the clinic is that you can do something about your fears and indeed about how you feel in any situation. It is not so much the situation as the way you think about it that produces feelings of anxiety or tension. By changing thoughts or attitudes, and by taking constructive actions such as deep breathing rather than continuing destructive behavior such as imagining impending disaster, you can change the way you feel in uncomfortable situations. It's easy, if you have this fear of flying, to become preoccupied with it, and essentially, worry yourself sick. Fearful fliers have to unlearn that tendency—you have to stop worrying and "think yourself well," as it were.

The Causes of Fear of Flying

The reasons why people are afraid of flying don't change the problem. If it's a control issue, fine. So what? For me, trying to identify the reasons for the fear of flying is a wild goose chase: Even if people know what caused the fear, it doesn't change the treatment. It's what they do about it is that's important.

I've worked with more than 500 fearful fliers, and they basically fall into three categories. The first includes people who have associated phobias. Claustrophobic individuals have a fear of confined spaces, so they can't handle lifts or tunnels or that sort of thing. Others have a fear of heights or an obsessive fear of dying.

A second group of fearful fliers are people whose life situation has precipitated the phobia—they were okay but suddenly things combined to overwhelm them. People in this group often develop their fear of flying after a divorce or the death of a parent. Women often experience it after they've had children: They feel all of the responsibility at once and develop a fear of dying and therefore leaving the children as orphans. For people in this group, there's some sort of a buildup of environmental stress or a combination of events—divorce, losing a job, whatever—any one of which they could cope with on its own. Yet, in combination, these events are the straw that breaks the camel's back. The person goes into stress overload. And it just happens that they have to take a flight at that inopportune time.

The third group of fearful fliers is made up of those who have had some sort of frightening or disturbing incident involving flying. They've been in an emergency landing, have experienced severe turbulence, or have had a relative die in a plane crash. They feel the fear as a result of a real-life incident involving a degree of real threat, and they need help to overcome that fear.

In spite of the differences between these groups, I honestly don't believe it makes any difference where the fear comes from, because ultimately everybody has to learn to think and behave differently. Obviously, what they've been doing in relation to flying hasn't been working.

The Nature of the Beast

Now, the expression "fear of flying" is really quite a misnomer. Fear is a realistic reaction to a real-life threat, which, in almost every case, the fear of flying is not. It's really a phobia, an irrational fearful reaction to an imagined or anticipated threat. No doubt there are risks involved with flying, but as we say in the course, the risks in traveling across the city in a car are so much greater than taking a dozen flights anywhere we want to go. In fact, the odds are very much on our side when we're up there.

When they're traveling in a car, people put those risks out of mind. They choose not to think about the fact that someone's mother was killed in a car or someone's father had his leg broken—and all the other horrible things that happen to people in cars. When it comes to flying, however, people often lose this sense of perspective, choosing instead to think about the risks and the aircraft accidents reported in the media. They overlook the hundreds of thousands of people flying at any moment in time and the myriad of uneventful flights that have taken place here and around the world today. Obviously, the evening news would be pretty boring if it reported all of this. But we have to be aware that, unless we also acknowledge the uneventful flights along with the accidents, a very distorted picture is created.

Chronic worriers—which is what most people with a flight phobia tend to be—follow the general rule that, when in doubt, they should assume the worst. They think, for example, "This will be the first plane in Qantas's history that will explode in midair, and I'll die in it." It's that sort of thinking—expecting the worst all the time and focusing on the negative.

Also, people who develop a fear of flying often have overactive imaginations. They think too much, and in self-destructive ways. They are their own worst enemies, sabotaging themselves with crazy thinking like the "what-if" game: What if I can't handle it? What if I go crazy? What if I freak out? What if I have a panic attack? What if the man next to me has a heart attack? What if the plane explodes? What if we hit turbulence? There's a tendency to anticipate everything and live in the future rather than concentrate on what's happening in the moment.

The best way to break through these fears is to deal with every moment and try to do whatever you can now to feel comfortable. You can cope with anything when and if it happens, but you don't have to try to do it all at once. People who worry about the past or anticipate the future inevitably end up spoiling the present, and that goes for a flight as well.

Taking Action

It's important to give yourself permission to be anxious. Anxiety is as much a part of living as depression, elation, arousal, anger, or any other feeling is—it's part of being alive. It's whether you allow yourself to be immobilized by anxiety and then what you do about the anxiety that's important. People sometimes become afraid of being afraid, anxious about being anxious. Fearful fliers and other worrying types often become self-conscious because they want to appear cool and in command and are frightened that their anxiety will show through—in fact, most of the time the people around them are totally oblivious to their fear.

The fundamental task is to refocus your thinking. You have to realize that you are not helpless in these situations—you need to be active rather than passive. Here there is a curious contradiction: If you can't relax naturally, then you have to work at it. It's no good sitting there telling yourself to "Relax!" or "Sleep!" You won't do it because you're tense and you're thinking of other things. What you can do instead is to change the channel: Do other things with your mind and then with your body that will help you to calm down.

Learning Coping Skills

Realistic thinking is the key to calming down. Physical relaxation is important, but ultimately, it's what you're doing with your mind that's most important. By changing the way you interpret situations, you can change the way you feel. Let's take turbulence, for example. What happens is that you feel the plane go bumpety-bumpety-bump, or drop, and you think, "It's going to drop out of the air! The wings are falling off! I'm going to throw up, I'm going to die, I'll never see the children again, they'll be orphans, their lives will be ruined." If you do this whole number on yourself, then of course you'll feel miserable, anxious, sad, frightened, spooked, and confused.

However, by adopting a different approach in that situation, you can remind yourself, "The plane is designed to do this and hundreds of thousands of planes have done it for seventy years or more. I'm uncomfortable, but I've been uncomfortable before and it was okay." It's like being in a car driving over a rough road. It's not pleasant, you'd rather not be there, but the car's designed to do it, so you tough it out and eventually get to your destination. The way you choose to respond to a situation determines how you feel about it.

As long as you're awake, you're always thinking, and so if you have a flight phobia you focus on the "what ifs": What if the engine stops? What if the pilot has a heart attack? What if the wings fall off? What if the passenger next to me is a terrorist? What if I have a panic attack on the plane? You can set up roadblocks in your mind to help yourself stop dwelling on the flight and stop playing the "what-if" game.

To stop sabotaging yourself, think of something else. Distract yourself with a book, the in-flight movie, or an activity such as crocheting, breathing deeply, or doing a whole stack of other things. For this purpose, along with the exercises we teach in the program, I suggest that you take a portable cassette player with music you enjoy on the flight with you. Likewise for books, crosswords, or work. It can also help to talk to the person next to you—anything to get your mind onto another subject.

When worriers focus on themselves, it feeds the fire of their anxieties: "Oh my God, what if? What if?" They become self-preoccupied and shut out the other things happening around them, sometimes building up a good bit of steam and freaking out. It's important to learn to control that and refocus. There are always other things to think about, particularly in a situation like a flight, when you're among many other people. You can look at them, try to imagine who they are, what they do, what the relationship is between this one and that one, or what they had for breakfast—anything to occupy your mind with other things and get you out of yourself.

I don't mean studying the cabin crew to see whether they look frightened, which is another thing that some people do. In reality, there's no way of knowing what they are feeling. Their expressions probably have nothing whatsoever to do with the aircraft, if the truth be known. It could be a difficult passenger they've just had a run-in with three seats up, but the problem with worriers in these situations is that they assume the worst. For example, they say, "See that tense expression on the flight attendant? Obviously there's a problem with the plane," instead of saying, "Oh, maybe she's having a hard day," or speculating that she's just broken up with her husband. Don't assume there's something wrong with the plane. The techniques and exercises below will help you get through your next flight if you learn them and practice them.

Deep Breathing

Changing the way in which you breathe can bring about a change in your physical condition very quickly, which in turn affects your psychological condition. To relax through deep breathing, first focus on each breath. Breathe in through your nose and out through your mouth. Try to fill your lungs like a taut balloon and then force all the air out when you exhale. Count 1–2–3–4–5 as you breathe in and 6–7–8–9–10 as you breathe out to help you slow down and take deeper breaths. Deep breathing adds oxygen to the blood, which has a physiological, calming effect on the brain.

Most of the time, deep breathing will be enough to help you feel calmer. Remember that since you have to breathe wherever you are, you can always choose to take deeper breaths and help yourself relax.

Working the Muscle Groups

If you're still feeling anxious after practicing deep breathing, then the next thing to do is to tense and relax as you breathe. Just tense lightly . . . and relax . . . tense . . . and relax. This is also very useful. It's doing two things: relaxing you physically and also focusing your mind on activity. That's the fundamental goal—directing your thinking into constructive channels, rather than letting it fall into self-defeating patterns.

Having a relaxation tape isn't important in and of itself. Lots of books about relaxation describe techniques, but really it's just a matter of systematically tensing and relaxing muscles throughout your body. Start with the muscles in the feet: Tense and relax these muscles and only these muscles. Light tension only. Then tense and relax them again, all the time maintaining the deep breathing pattern. Then move to the muscles in the lower leg and tense and relax these muscles a couple of times. Repeat this procedure for the muscles in the thighs, then the buttocks, and the groin.

Once you've worked through the lower body, tense all the muscles below the waist and relax them. Take a deep breath, focus your mind, and then let it wander, checking to see if any of the muscles are still tight when you want them relaxed. Imagine smoothing away any residual tension. Then repeat the tensing and relaxing with the muscles in the stomach, followed by the chest, shoulders, lower back, upper arms and lower arms, and finishing up with the hands. Once you're done, take a deep breath, tense all the muscles in the upper body, and then relax. Let your mind wander again, check the muscles for any remaining tension and smooth it away.

Finally, tense and relax the muscles in the neck, face, and scalp. Once you've done that, take a big deep breath, then tense and relax *all* the muscles in your body, from the top of your head to the tips of your toes. Take a big deep breath, and let your mind scan your body and check out all those muscles to see if there is any tension in them. Then try to soothe away that tension. Imagine the muscles relaxing.

People sometimes have trouble doing physical relaxation exercises because they are perfectionists and want to get it right or because they tense their muscles so hard that they become uncomfortable. All that's necessary is gentle tensing and relaxing—you don't have to turn purple in the face. And you should be careful if a part of your body is particularly sensitive. For example, if you're given to migraines, then it's probably not a good idea to fool around with the muscles in your head and neck.

Mental Relaxation

In addition to physical relaxation techniques, there are also ways that you can calm your mind. As I said before, you need to change the channel from the horror movie to the calm and soothing channel. You can create these calming images for yourself. One method is to imagine waves breaking on the shore as you breathe deeply. As you breathe in, the wave laps on the shore. As you breathe out, the wave recedes, leaving you feeling more and more relaxed.

Another technique involves imagining a place where you feel safe, secure, and quite relaxed. This can be a favorite room in your childhood home, your current home, your parents' home, or a friend's house. It doesn't matter where it is, as long as you feel safe and calm in that place. Create the room in your mind, focusing all your attention on picturing its details: the shape and size of the room, the doors and windows, the patterns of light and shade, the furniture and other objects, and the colors, textures, and any smells or sounds you associate with the room. Because the goal is to focus your thoughts on a calming image, if your mind wanders, just say gently to yourself, "Stop," and think yourself back into your safe place.

If you prefer, you might imagine a place outdoors where you feel comfortable and safe: in a valley beside a river, on a mountaintop watching the sunset, or on a cliff overlooking waves breaking on the rocks below. The important thing that all the techniques do is bring about a change in consciousness. They change the way you breathe and help you focus your thoughts on something other than flying.

Desensitization

The Fearless Flyers program gradually desensitizes you to the feared situation, exposing you increasingly to planes, airports, and other aspects of flying. Ultimately the class does the graduation flight and you experience the whole thing at once. Over an eight-week period of desensitization, you smell the aircraft, you walk around in the aircraft, and learn about the aircraft. You're physically desensitizing yourself.

Another procedure can help you get through a flight and can be combined with the relaxation techniques. Write all the various stages involved in making a flight on cards: making the reservations, packing, going to the airport, checking in, boarding the plane. Then put them into an order called a "desensitization hierarchy," from least feared activity to most feared activity. It doesn't have to be in a logical or chronological order, just the order from the least frightening to the most frightening.

You may feel comfortable in every flight-related activity except turbulence. If that's the case, what you do is imagine each of those stages on the cards, and if you feel calm, proceed to the next one until you start to feel anxious. Then do the relaxation techniques to help yourself imagine being calm in that situation. Once you feel relaxed, stop at that point and then work though the cards again from the beginning until you are able to imagine each of the stages of the flight without experiencing any anxiety.

It Takes Time

I try to emphasize in the course that fearful fliers can change if they want to—they can do something about the problem. As we say in each course, "We can't fly for you." You have to do your own flying, breathing, or whatever. But we can show you ways that help people calm down and feel a greater degree of comfort. All I aim for is to help people be more comfortable on their next flights, more in control of themselves, and active rather than passive. Now that doesn't necessarily mean they'll be whistling and skipping up and down the aisles. But many people become quite happy on the plane. They have resolved the issue. With others, it takes more time. Just as you have to practice if you want to perfect your golf swing, you have to keep working at beating your fear of flying.

By the time people take the step of seeing a psychologist or joining a fear-of-flying program, they've spent a long time practicing the negative. They come in with five, ten, or twenty years' history of worry. With all those years of practice behind them, they've become pretty good worriers, so they can't expect to turn it around quickly. Change generally occurs slowly and can be progressive. As long as there is movement in the direction of progress, then that's fine.

If there is a sudden transformation, and suddenly you lose the fear—that's great. But don't throw your hands up in the air and say, "Oh God, I knew it wouldn't work," if the next flight isn't the easiest one you've ever had. It just means you have to keep on working at being more relaxed.

THE DEMONS WITHIN: STUART SPENCE'S STORY

My palms get sweaty, and I'll get fidgety.
It's a fear of the unknown.

—Peter McGee
fearful flier, New Canaan, Connecticut

S tuart Spence had an unusual request the night his Fearless Flyers
class was touring the Qantas training facilities for flight attendants.
As the rest of his classmates were filing out of the model of a jet's
interior that is used for training exercises, Spence asked his instructors if
he could be left alone in the darkened "plane" with the door shut.

The experiment was more relevant than anyone else suspected at
the time, perhaps even Spence himself. For while he was aware that the
trigger for his terror had been the moment that the flight attendants shut
the doors of the plane, the realization was dawning on Spence that his
feeling of being trapped had more to do with what had gone wrong with
his life than with anything related to flying. "My fear of flying was a
manifestation of a whole lot of other problems in my life," explains
Spence, a thirty-seven-year-old photographer from Sydney who special-
izes in celebrity portraits. "My wife was going through a breakdown, and
I hadn't known about it—our marriage was breaking up. I had mortgage
pressure, I wasn't happy in my work. I felt trapped, and I was doing things
I didn't want to do."

For years, Spence loved to travel; for him, getting on a plane rep-
resented freedom and fun. He flew often for work, mostly round-trips
from Sydney to Melbourne, about an hour away by jet. All that changed
one morning when Spence was boarding a ten-seater plane en route to a
job in Merimbula, a coastal town in southern New South Wales. "I
couldn't get on," he remembers. "I was nauseous; I was dizzy. I just did
not want to be there. My brain was screaming, 'Get off this sucker!'"

Sadly, the seed was sown. Spence stopped flying altogether and
started taking long-distance trains for business trips. The irony of his situation was not lost on him. "I would get a sleeper, and there I would be
in a very small room for eight hours—on a train!" he chuckles. "That
seemed to be okay with my higher self, but for some reason, an airplane

wasn't." Worse than the inconvenience, though, was the emotional help-lessness Spence was experiencing. "I felt as if my power had been taken away," he says. "I didn't feel like a whole person anymore. Traveling had been a large part of my psyche, and when it was taken away, I felt hopeless."

The good news, however, was that Spence, grounded by his fears, had to take stock of his life. He first sought recovery through hypnosis and a series of natural remedies. He then turned to a doctor who was "an anxiety guru," and pronounced that a flop. He eventually turned to existential therapy, which emphasizes "here and now" interactions and feelings, rather than past events and rational thinking. This therapy was "a way to assess and tackle what was going on in my life," as Spence puts it, and he considers it crucial to his recovery. "Because I was so driven to succeed in this thing, there was nothing I wouldn't do for the cause."

If the therapy was the brains of his recovery, the Fearless Flyers course was the brawn, Spence says. When his mother heard about the course on the radio and told him about it, he checked into it and was pleased to find out that the course covered psychology and relaxation training. For Spence knew that he actually loved the process of flying—if he could only get there. "Sitting down in the plane and seeing the flight attendant close the door, I felt there was no way out," he says. "That if I didn't escape now . . ."

He pauses. "What would happen if I didn't escape was the unknown anxiety," he speculates.

During the Fearless Flyers course, Spence concentrated on taking back the power he had always had but had lost sight of and on having more control over the actions of his life and his emotions. "You have to work for this and train your mind," he says of the relaxation training in the course. "It's like going back to school." He also began to think about the flights he'd been unable to get on and look deeper at what they had meant to him. "My destinations coincided with incredible anxiety," he explains. "I'd be going to Melbourne to do a photo shoot I didn't want to do at five in the morning with a bunch of people I didn't want to go with—all to earn money to pay for a mortgage I didn't want to be part of."

During the last Fearless Flyers session before the graduation flight, when he and his classmates took turns summing up what they'd gotten out of the course, Spence announced, "I reintroduced myself to my own power—it's unstoppable if you can tap into it." When it was time to board the graduation flight from Sydney to Melbourne, he selected a window seat and didn't flinch when the doors were closed.

"Somewhere along the line, I'd given myself permission to make it all okay again, so I was dandy," he says. Adds Spence, "Conquering a fear that you think is insurmountable is very powerful. It made me wonder what else I could do."

Indeed, when I caught up with Spence a few months after he'd finished the course, he was out of his marriage and had sold his house. He had also cut back on his photography business and was starting an acting career. "In other words, I've tried to follow the bliss," he says, referring to the saying from Joseph Campbell. "The river that runs inside you knows where it's supposed to get to. If you put dams up with bad mortgages, bad jobs, and bad marriages, and you don't deal with those things, the water starts making other strange detours around the dam, and there's a big backlog behind this dam—all this pressure you feel. Finally I threw my hands up in the air and said, 'I'm not happy doing this,' and changed every one of the things that was bugging me.

"I think it's incredibly misguided for fearful fliers to place all the blame simply on the airplane and the dangers of flying," he concludes. "In doing so, one runs the risk of putting a finger in the dam, just patching it up and saying, 'Everything's okay now!'"

After a lot of work on himself inside and outside the Fearless Flyers course, Spence is flying happily again—and often. The changes he made in his life helped him ease the apprehensions underlying his fear of flying. His message to fearful fliers who may be experiencing a transference of anxieties from other parts of their lives is a powerful one. "A lot of people desperately need to talk about what's going on in their lives," he says.

"THIS IS YOUR CAPTAIN": WHAT YOU WANTED TO KNOW BUT COULDN'T ASK

[Flying felt like] a faceless experience. When you get on a bus, you can see the bus driver. When you get in a cab, you can see the cab driver. On a plane, you can't see the crew, just the enormous jet and those little windows up front. It felt as if they weren't human.

—Richard Hardwick
Fearless Flyers class of November 1992

Because fearful fliers are so unfamiliar with what goes on behind the door to the flight deck, a vital part of the Fearless Flyers aviation education is a talk by a Qantas captain and an opportunity for class members to ask him or her directly about their areas of concern. It also allows them to perceive the person flying them through the stratosphere as a competent, flesh-and-blood human being who cares as much as they do that the flight goes without incident.

This is why it is a good idea for recovering fearful fliers to ask to visit the cockpit during a flight. In fact, I still do so to maintain my recovery. Visits during the flight are permitted during some international flights if a request is made through a flight attendant, who will then escort a passenger to the flight deck if it's a convenient time for the crew. In the U.S., FAA regulations forbid in-flight visits for security reasons. In these cases, as soon as I step on the plane, I duck out of the way of the people filing in behind me and ask to say hello to the flight crew before the plane leaves the gate. When I step into the cockpit, I always identify myself as a recovering fearful flier and ask the crew questions about the flight, usually about the kind of takeoff we're going to have— if it will be sharp or gradual, if the power will be cut back during the initial climb, if we will be making any sharp turns. Sometimes I'll ask about the weather en route. Every pilot I've encountered, on no matter what airline, has been welcoming and happy to answer questions or discuss the aircraft they were flying that day.

It helps to hear reassuring explanations of topics that trigger your fears, straight from the source. Qantas Captain Lyn Williams, who speaks to Fearless Flyers classes when he's not piloting 747s, here addresses the subjects that fearful fliers in the course ask him the most about during his lectures and subsequent question-and-answer periods.

THE PILOT'S PERSPECTIVE, WITH LYN WILLIAMS, QANTAS CAPTAIN

Recurrent Training

Pilots go through extensive training, and it doesn't just stop when they graduate from flight school. As required by Qantas, recurrent, or continuing, pilot training has to satisfy all the requirements for maintaining an air transport pilot's license and command instrument rating. But beyond the statutory requirements of various aviation licenses, the purpose of recurrent training is to give pilots the opportunity to practice how to handle any non-normal events—such as a rejected takeoff—that could happen in the course of a flight, even if the chance is infinitesimal. The recurrent training is also based on the requirements of Australia's Civil Aviation Authority, plus any additional airline requirements. These could include any scenarios not normally experienced in day-to-day flying or expected in a lifetime of flying, from tire failures to a passenger running amok.

To maintain a license, a pilot must successfully complete four sessions of four hours each per year in an approved training program in a simulator. (Simulator requirements differ with countries and airlines—some airlines, for example, require fewer but lengthier sessions.) A simulator is a very sophisticated piece of machinery duplicating the layout of an airplane's flight deck. It has flight controls to fly the airplane, including the control column, which controls the elevators in the fore and aft (up and down) direction, and ailerons, which turn the aircraft left or right; instruments to monitor the aircraft's integrity and navigation; and switches to turn systems on and off, all of which respond in exactly the same way as in the airplane. The simulator has movement in six axes, or directions, and visual displays of all of the airports you'll be flying to. It allows a multitude of non-normal procedures to be simulated and is preferred for training exercises because it only costs between US $16 million and US $20 million, compared to between US $150 million and US $200 million for a real airplane. Likewise, it costs approximately US $650 to US $1,000 per hour to operate, compared to between US $10,000 and US $15,000 to operate an airplane.

The pilot also must complete annual route check requirements. These entail having an examining officer, or "check captain," fly with the crew and observe the operation en route and the pilot to make sure he or she is operating correctly in the everyday commercial environment.

*A flight simulator is a replica of a jet's flight deck and controls,
such as that of a real Boeing 777 shown here.*

The pilot also must attend a complete emergency procedures session every year. This entails one or two days at the ground school enacting emergency evacuations in various scenarios, such as on land. Ditching emergencies, such as that in which a plane has overshot a runway and landed in water, are also practiced. It is a requirement of both the Australian and American flight authorities that the technical and cabin crew be able to evacuate a full aircraft, with only half the cabin doors in use, within ninety seconds!

Apart from the recurrent checks previously mentioned, the crews may be subject to spot checks from time to time to ensure that the airline's high standard is maintained. This is even another layer of the checking and training systems within the airline, designed to guarantee that the standard is met.

Frequency of Simulator Training

A pilot's four required visits to the simulator for recurrent training may be supplemented by additional visits when he or she supports the training of another pilot. All sessions are flown as if flying an airplane in real life, with the standard crew of captain, first officer, and flight engineer, if the simulator is for an older-model 747 that carries a flight engineer. Endorsement training—a license to fly a particular aircraft—or promotional training—instruction to attain a higher rank—requires at least twelve sessions. Also, for what is called recency requirements, a pilot must maintain skills for takeoff, landing, and instrument flying. So if a pilot has been on holiday or absent because of sickness and has not flown in the preceding thirty-five days, he or she must update recency requirements in the simulator.

During my thirty-one years of flying since I began as a Qantas cadet, or pilot trainee, in 1967, I'd estimate that, with license renewals every year, crew supports, endorsements, promotional training, and all the other sundry reasons for training, I've flown in the simulator at least 200 times.

Medical Checks

Medical checks are completed at least once a year, depending upon age, and they are quite thorough, often including blood tests, electrocardiograms, lung capacity tests, and eyesight and hearing tests. Presently, the medical standard of a pilot is measured according to a point system adding up to fourteen. The idea is to accumulate less than fourteen points; points accumulate according to age, family medical history, and current medical fitness. At the maximum fourteen points, a stress electrocardiogram is required. Depending on medical status, a pilot may be allowed to regain acceptable status by exercising or engaging in certain medical procedures or treatments. For example, a pilot can fly again after bypass surgery, but only if a heart attack has not already occurred. A pilot must retire if he or she has a heart attack, but the ongoing medical checks tend to warn pilots of problems before a heart attack happens. The bottom line is that if a pilot is not fit, he or she is not allowed to fly.

Roles of Flight Crew Members

To sum up the roles of the flight crew, the captain is the overall commander of the aircraft, responsible for correct navigation and operation of the aircraft to ensure the safety of the passengers, aircraft, crew, and freight. The first officer is a pilot licensed to be a deputy captain. The second officer is a pilot used for support at cruising altitudes to allow the captain or first officer to have a rest — but the captain or first officer must be "pilot of the watch" when the other is resting and a second officer is providing support duties. Also, the captain and first officer are always at the controls during takeoff, landing, and at an altitude of less than 5,000 feet (1,524 meters).

A flight engineer is used on older 747s, such as the 100, 200, or 300 models, to monitor fuel, air-conditioning, hydraulics, pressurization, and thrust control. Newer planes, such as the 747-400 or 767 have computers to do this job. It is possible for a flight engineer to become a pilot or vice versa. The roles are not normally interchangeable, although the second officer is trained and licensed to give in-flight relief to the flight engineer on older 747s. In the U.S., captains over the age of sixty can retrain to be flight engineers, as by law pilots in Australia as well as the U.S. have to retire as captains at sixty. The retirement age for a captain can vary by country — it is fifty-five in the U.K. and Germany, for example.

Flight Time Limitations

There are various legal and industry requirements regarding flight time limitations for pilots. Limitations vary according to whether the crew includes two, three, or four pilots (and a flight engineer on the older 747s). Other additional requirements are whether the aircraft in question has a horizontal crew rest or private place where a member of the crew can lie down and rest or sleep.

A two-pilot crew — a captain and first officer — cannot exceed eight hours of flight deck time, or time when they're behind the controls. With a three- or four-pilot crew, which includes an additional pilot for relief during longer flights, each pilot can have up to eight and a half hours on the flight deck or at the controls. However, a crew's total tour of duty can be up to eleven to sixteen hours, with extensions of one to three and a half hours, depending on the number of crew. That time is measured from the time that you report for duty, and for the short time after a flight that is required for debriefing. These limitations may be even greater, depending upon factors such as the number of two-person flight hours per pilot in the previous week, number of hours flown in the past thirty days, and number of hours flown in the past year. The final responsibility lies with the individual, who must ensure that he or she is fit and sufficiently rested before flying. This is required by law.

Alcohol and Drug Regulations

Australian law dictates that alcohol not be consumed by a member of the crew within eight hours of the time he or she reports for duty. An individual must ensure that he or she is fit for flying. For example, if a pilot has enjoyed the excesses of a Christmas party, more time would be needed before flying. Qantas and the Flight Crew Association have established an alcohol and drug program for flight crew members, so any flight crew member who is suspected of having an alcohol or drug problem is encouraged to seek diagnosis and to follow through with treatment. In doing so, they will not jeopardize job security or promotional opportunities, and as with any illness, their medical records will be treated in the strictest confidence. This is generally true throughout the industry.

All crew and airline personnel are alert to any substance abuse, as they are all concerned about work performance and safety. Some airlines and countries even have spot checks. Any abuse of the law entails an immediate license suspension and possible termination of employment.

The Age of Your Pilot

The silver-haired, distinguished male pilot as pictured in the movies is now quite rare. Looks, a mature age, and a flamboyant personality are not prerequisites to becoming a pilot, although some do try to live up to the image! These days, it is possible that your pilot will be younger than the stereotype—or female.

In pilot selection, strict training and promotional requirements are the order of the day. Every pilot is recruited on the basis of his or her potential to become a captain. A pilot at Qantas only will be passed if he or she can maintain a level of proficiency far above the statutory requirements. Very few aspiring pilots make it into an airline, so you can rest assured that if you see a pilot in his or her twenties, they've earned their positions with hard work and ability.

At Qantas, no matter the number of flight hours or previous experience, each new pilot begins a career as a second officer. He or she has to pass all the training steps right from the beginning. Even high-ranking pilots from the air force and captains and first officers from other airlines must achieve the statutory requirements in all ranks before becoming a Qantas captain.

Quality of Commuter Airline Pilots

Some pilots, to avoid long flying hours and time away from home, prefer the life of a commuter pilot. Commuter pilots have strict licensing requirements as well and are subject to checks from the FAA in the U.S. and the Civil Aviation Authority in Australia. Most commuter airlines are associated with large commercial airlines, so their safety records reflect upon those of the bigger carriers. Hence, there is a further interest for an airline, apart from complying with federal regulations, to ensure that commuter airlines have high safety standards.

A Four-Engine Failure

In the most unlikely chance that all four engines on a jet fail, the aircraft can glide quite a considerable distance. For example, at an average cruising altitude of 35,000 feet (10,671 meters), a 747-400 will glide in excess of 140 miles (220 kilometers). The time for its descent would be at least twenty minutes. During this time, either the automatic start function of the engine or the pilot's intervention would have the engines operating with little loss of height or time.

Many years ago, in separate incidents, aircraft from two different airlines each lost engine thrust, due to the unexpected hazard of volcanic ash, which prevented the engines from receiving sufficient pure air to operate normally. Both aircraft successfully regained power well above the ground. (More information on one of these flights is given on page 96, in the chapter on weather.) Volcanic activities are now constantly monitored worldwide, with updates by satellite. Flight into volcanic ash can now be avoided, so this should never again cause a problem.

All airplanes are basically gliders with engines for propulsion. Regardless of the number of engines, the same principles apply to gliding distance. It's important to realize that it would be a one-in-a-million chance for an engine to fail, let alone for two to fail at the same time. Aircraft the size of a 747-400 at a weight of 620,000 pounds (281,818 kilograms)—220,000 pounds (100,000 kilograms) heavier than a 767 aircraft at its maximum takeoff weight—can continue to maintain a height of 8,000 feet (2.43 kilometers) above sea level on one engine.

The Plane's Equilibrium

People walking around inside the airplane will not upset its balance. To give you an idea, a 747-400 has a maximum takeoff weight of nearly 875,000 pounds (397,727 kilograms)—that includes the weight of the plane, passengers, fuel, and cargo combined. A person normally weighs about 155 to 175 pounds, or 70 to 80 kilograms. Even a person weighing 240 pounds (120 kilograms) would have an insignificant effect as he or she moved around the cabin.

The fuel tank in the tail of the aircraft contains up to 22,000 pounds (9,900 kilograms) of fuel on long flights. (The 747-400 can carry approximately 378,400 pounds [170,280 kilograms] of fuel in all of its fuel tanks.) This 22,000 pounds in the tail weighs about the same amount as 120 passengers. During flight, this fuel is transferred about 100 feet forward in the aircraft to the center wing tanks. The wing tanks—fuel tanks within each wing—carry up to 121,000 pounds (54,450 kilograms) on each side, while the center wing tank under the cabin floor in the center of the aircraft can carry up to 114,000 pounds (51,300 kilograms). Except for 19,800 to 22,000 pounds (8,910 to 9,900 kilograms) of reserve fuel, the rest of the large weight in fuel is moved by pumps from these fuel tanks via fuel manifolds, or piping, to be burned by the engines. The aircraft compensates for this transfer of weight with its automatic trim feature, in which a computer adjusts the flight controls to keep the aircraft on its required path. Compared to this, passengers moving around the aircraft are totally insignificant.

On small airplanes, the size of the airplane and the number of passengers must be balanced, but within the realms of practicality, all aircraft can be trimmed with the weight on board. If the aircraft has been loaded correctly, it should be no problem to compensate for the movement of passengers in the cabin. Airlines train load control officers to oversee the correct loading of aircraft, so this does not become a problem. At Qantas, every bag or piece of freight is bar-coded, so the computer knows its weight and where it is loaded.

Water Landings

The chance of an aircraft like the 747 or 767 ditching, or making a water landing, in the ocean is so remote that one should count on a win at the lottery first. I cannot see any reason for ditching unless the airplane ran out of fuel, and this should never be a possibility. But even if an aircraft did land in the water, model flotation tests of Boeing 377 Strata-Cruisers, KC-97 refueling tankers, and Russian TU-124s indicate that successful water landings are possible.

Once an Asia-based airline had a plane that overran terra firma during a takeoff in Hong Kong because the pilot found he had more runway behind him than ahead. The plane ended up competing with the ferries on Hong Kong Harbor! Nobody was killed, and this aircraft remained in the water for quite some time—days, in fact. The inference here is that there is quite a lot of buoyancy in the aircraft due to the size of the fuel tanks, and quite often a lot of air is trapped in the fuel tanks and compartments on either side. Also, the cargo holds would support the buoyancy of the aircraft. The cause of this mishap was pilot error; nothing was wrong with the plane.

Clear Air Turbulence

Clear air turbulence cannot be seen on our instruments. As the name implies, this type of turbulence occurs in clear air and cannot be seen visually or on radar. Weather radar picks up thunderstorms, which we can assume will cause some turbulence, due to the instability in the air forming the clouds. But clear air turbulence is more of a hazard because it can come without warning. For that reason, it's our company policy to ensure that all passengers wear their seat belts when seated.

This type of turbulence usually occurs when we fly from one type of weather pattern into another, for example, from a relatively slow-moving air mass (10 to 20 knots) into or near a jet stream, where wind speeds can be well above 100 knots. Fortunately, incidents of severe clear air turbulence involving injury to passengers are relatively rare. But you can be sure that as a passenger, just like those of us on the flight deck, you will not be hurt if you are wearing your seat belt.

Microbursts and Wind Shear

A microburst is a meteorological phenomenon normally associated with thunderstorms or extreme frontal systems, causing a strong downward rush of air out of a cloud, with its outburst of severe winds on or near the ground lasting only one to five minutes. In the past, microbursts have caused planes to crash as they were taking off or on their approach for landing. We know much more about microbursts than we used to, and special computers have been designed to warn aircraft of possible microburst activity.

Wind shear is another adverse weather condition. Wind is mainly horizontal at altitudes below 500 feet (150 meters). However, as a plane descends during its approach for landing or climbs out after takeoff, it can fly into horizontal air masses moving at different speeds to the one it has left. This change is known as shear. The greater the change in wind speed, the greater the fluctuation in aircraft speed and possibility of turbulence and flight path deviation. However, some aircraft, such as the 747-400, have an instrument that warns us of wind shear. This computer both gives us an announced warning—"Wind shear, wind shear, wind shear"—and shows the positive climb indication on our primary flight display instrument so that we can climb safely away from the ground. As well, we are vigilant to basic indications on our flight instruments showing any unacceptable flight path deviations and any abnormalities in speed, attitude, thrust, or altitude.

Flight crews take three kinds of actions in regard to wind shear and microbursts: avoidance, precautions, and recovery. Pilots want to arrive safely as much as the passengers do, so they assess all available information, such as reports by other pilots of wind shear and turbulence, and weather reports, including data for the area immediately around the airport. We avoid problems by delaying approach or takeoff, diverting to another airport, or using another runway. That runway would be at a safe distance from the original runway and the offending microburst or wind shear.

If there is not any substantial evidence of wind shear conditions, but the pilot suspects it because of past experience in that area or under those conditions, as a precaution, we would change runways and if necessary use reserves available in engine thrust and climbing ability, which we call "flying at optimum performance." And whenever flight path deviations become unacceptable, pilots are trained to recover by performing a terrain avoidance procedure: making an immediate go-around, which means aborting the approach and landing and climbing away from terrain.

Thunderstorms

Thunderstorms normally have very little effect on planes, especially because pilots can avoid them. If for some reason an aircraft does have to fly close to a thunderstorm, or even through it, they are structurally strong enough to withstand even the huge forces in major storms, much higher forces than those the human body could withstand. During the early days of the 747, Boeing deliberately tried to destroy a plane to see how strong it was. One of the tests involved using a hydraulic ram to bend the wingtip of the airplane. Before the wing broke, it had bent more than 22 feet (6.7 meters) above and below its static position! As you can tell, although it is much better to avoid disrupting the meal service by flying around in thunderstorms, the aircraft is easily able to withstand the forces inside a storm.

Lightning often comes with thunderstorms and is also not seriously dangerous. When an aircraft is struck by lightning, it causes no harm to the aircraft or passengers, because every metallic part of the aircraft is wired together to allow a continual flow of electricity until the electricity can find the easiest place to exit the aircraft.

Takeoffs and Landings in Fog

An aircraft can take off or land safely in fog. In fact, the visibility requirements for modern aircraft are the lowest they've ever been; aircraft can even land in zero visibility, using the aircraft's automatic landing system, onboard computers, and constant information from sophisticated landing signals and radio beams from the ground. The pilots also monitor the approach to ensure operational integrity. In fact, any airplane with the required onboard equipment and trained crew can land in zero visibility at any airport with the required ground equipment. But this equipment is expensive to maintain, so it is used only by planes that fly to fog-prone airports. (Commercial aircraft do not use an automatic system for takeoff.)

For all approaches where visibility is less than 800 meters or the base of the clouds is less than 200 feet (60 meters) above the ground, Qantas requires automatic landings. We monitor the approach and look for visual clues of the runway. If at any time the autopilots are not functioning correctly, we take over and go around. The pilot can override the autopilot at any time—not vice versa!

A decision height is the height above the ground at which the decision must be made either to land or abort the landing. Qantas has a decision height of 20 feet (6 meters) on the radio altimeter and 100 meters (330 feet) forward visibility, which means at the 20-foot radio altimeter height, the pilot should be able to see at least 100 meters ahead. This should enable him or her to see enough runway lighting to make a safe landing with the autopilot engaged. At the decision height of twenty feet, if the required visibility is not available to land the aircraft safely, the pilot will execute an immediate "missed approach" and climb away from the terrain. At that point the pilot will get a revised forecast from the meteorology office to see whether conditions might improve at that airport, and provided the plane has enough fuel, he or she may remain in the area until the visibility improves. The pilot may also choose to continue on to an alternate airport.

Bird Strikes

I cannot recollect an occasion in modern flying with modern aircraft and large modern engines that birds alone caused a plane to crash. In fact, the certification of the modern jet engine is quite spectacular. One of the tests involves throwing different-sized defrosted birds, from geese down to small birds, into the mouth of the engine. The engine must maintain 75 percent takeoff thrust for ten minutes. Needless to say, the birds would be a little the worse for wear.

About fifteen to eighteen months ago, an aircraft taking off from New Zealand flew through a flock of birds. Once the aircraft returned to the airport—quite safely—about ninety carcasses were discovered at the far end of the runway.

Airline Regulatory Authorities

The airline regulatory authorities—such as the FAA and the Civil Aviation Authority—set regulations to ensure that airlines and aircraft are operated safely. They make sure that all pilots, airlines, and aircraft meet the very strict standards required by the aviation world.

As regulatory authorities, they ensure compliance of rules involving airworthiness of aircraft, crew licensing, and safety of operation, even while airlines are operating in foreign territory. Their role is wide, covering airspace management, civil aviation orders and regulations, and any publications covering a vast range of requirements for the owners and operators of the airlines. They often spot-check to ensure compliance.

Judging Airline Safety

Air travel is the safest means of transport, statistically safer than crossing the road or even living in your own home. But purely because of the nature of human beings, of course, some airlines and some pilots are better and safer than others. Fortunately, aircraft manufacturers build in safety and warning systems to compensate for the possible weaknesses of pilots.

If aircraft are well maintained, all airlines with the same types of aircraft should be equal in safety. However, some airlines spend more time and money on pilot training, maintenance, and aircraft refurbishment than others. Education, cultural background, and economics all affect the efficiency of an airline.

So why buy a car from one salesperson and not another? Why choose one brand of television and not another? It is your choice, and that goes for airlines, too. You must choose an airline with which you are comfortable. Safety, training, reliability, schedule, and quality of service always come at a price. This needs to be considered if you base your choice of airline on the lowest fares. To get insight into which are the better airlines, pay attention to media reports and assess reactions of your friends who travel.

Checking for Contaminated Fuel

The major contaminant in fuel is usually water, which can get in there by rain or by fuel evaporation and dilute the fuel. As in a car, a plane engine doesn't combust water, only fuel. Yet fuel companies have very strict checking systems to ensure that the fuel for aircraft operations is pure. Furthermore, before every flight, ground engineers must check to ensure that there is no water in the fuel of each plane. This is known as "dipping the tanks," or draining a quantity of fuel from each aircraft tank and testing it for impurities or water.

Reserve Fuel

How much reserve fuel each plane carries varies depending on the weather requirements of the destination airport, but there's always sufficient fuel on board at any stage of flight to land at a suitable airport. If the weather conditions at the destination airport are poor, the plane carries extra fuel to cover all the contingencies. If for some reason the weather forecast was good but the conditions turn out to be poor, we would divert to a suitable alternate airport. At every stage of the flight, there are always sufficient reserves of fuel to make a safe landing at the required airport.

Rating — or Not Rating — Different Airports

In all honesty, there's no airport that I hate to fly into. Hong Kong's Kai Tak Airport is exciting because it's different and certainly gives the passengers an exhilarating view when approaching from the northwest to the southeast. The aircraft flies low over the buildings in Kowloon, where at times passengers swear that they are actually looking up at the washing hanging from the buildings in the surrounding hills and can see the TV programs in the lounge rooms! Apart from the excitement, it is a safe approach. (This airport was replaced by a newer one in July 1998.)

Los Angeles is a different type of airport because it's very busy. Pilots flying into Los Angeles are aware of the density of the traffic and take that into consideration on takeoff and landing.

Every airline requires that pilots are familiar with the airports they fly into, so there should never be an airport that a passenger should fear because it's "worse" than another. Airports like Hong Kong do require simulator sessions so that all types of approaches can be practiced. Also, an actual flight to Hong Kong is required, with a supervising captain, before a pilot is allowed to fly unsupervised into Hong Kong.

Investigating Accidents

The immediate response from the aviation industry to a fatal crash is a desire to find out why it happened, mainly because any accident reflects badly on the industry. This is true in spite of the fact that flying in an airplane is the safest means of transport. For example, in Australia, you could fly every day for twenty years, and the likelihood is that you would never have an accident — where there is damage to the aircraft or injury or death to passengers — or an incident, which is a non-life-threatening occurrence such as a bird strike or tire deflation.

When an accident occurs, we are anxious to find out the result of the investigation as soon as possible, because something may have caused it that we are not yet aware of. Unfortunately, the media are inclined to exaggerate the story to sell broadcast time or newspapers. Quite often the facts are exaggerated to such an extent that it takes a while for the truth to be displayed, even inside the aviation industry. Our safety and training departments join all the other watchdogs in the industry to ensure that every incident and accident is meticulously analyzed. We seek preventative ways to avoid accidents, study procedures, and reanalyze techniques. Airlines are continually in touch with aircraft and engine manufacturers to seek any improvement to the components that can be developed.

The airline industry is all about safety. In fact, Qantas's policy is "safety before schedule." We must achieve and maintain efficiency of operations and comfort of passengers with this policy in mind, so that, although we strive to be on schedule, we do not compromise safety. If an aircraft is not completely ready for flight, we remain on the ground until it is fixed. Safety is not an accident!

YOU'RE IN GOOD HANDS: THE AUTHOR OBSERVES A CREW UNDER PRESSURE

*When my wife and I go somewhere and
leave the kids at home, we almost always
take separate planes.*

—Brian Kinahan
fearful flier, Chapel Hill, North Carolina

H aving decided to see for myself how pilots are kept on their toes,
I'm sitting in the cockpit behind Qantas First Officer Bruce Milne.
Milne is licensed to be a deputy captain, so he has switched roles
with Captain Ian Emery at the controls of a 747-300 jumbo jet. We're
coming in for a landing at Hong Kong's Kai Tak Airport in very poor
visibility, and one of the jet's four engines fails.

The situation seems touch and go. The jet has almost reached
"minima," or "decision height," the altitude at which First Officer
Milne must decide whether to land or to abort the landing. To top it off,
Hong Kong is a complex airport where a plane must swoop down at an
angle, fly through part of the city, and land on a runway that extends
into the harbor. This approach has so little margin for error that, if you
happen to land there on a sunny day, you can look out the window and
see the pictures on television sets inside apartment buildings.

Today, there is no such visibility. And when an "outboard" (outside) engine fails, causing the jet to roll slightly, I sit in one of the two
observers' seats at the back of the cockpit and shudder. To First Officer
Milne and the rest of the crew, however, handling malfunctions is second
nature. Milne rectifies the roll by adjusting the rudder, which is located
on the tail of the plane and has the same effect as that on a boat, and
disconnects the autopilot, an action that automatically activates a siren
in the cockpit to alert the crew. As Captain Emery feeds him crucial
information on the flight's altitude and distance from the airport, Milne
aborts the landing. He follows the standard practice of making a go-
around while the shut-down procedures are carried out on the failed
engine, double-checking all systems to ensure that nothing else besides
the engine failure has gone wrong that might affect the safety of the
landing.

As the plane suddenly shifts from the posture of imminent landing to a climb, the roar of the remaining three engines is so intense that it's hard to believe the jet is using only a little more power than it would during a normal takeoff, which is, in turn, only about 75 percent of the power the plane can produce. Milne circles and makes another approach into the airport, landing without further incident this time.

This cockpit and the movements of the jet, especially the push back that I feel as the jet climbs, are so convincing that it's easy to forget that we have not even left the Sydney airport. We are, in fact, strapped into a AUS $15 million (US $9.7 million) 747-300 flight simulator at Qantas's airport headquarters, one of a fleet of eleven machines simulating various jet types. Boxy machines on stilts trailing hydraulic lines that help induce motion, they look like creatures out of *War of the Worlds* from the outside. Inside the cockpit, which even has interchangeable views depending on which airport you want to fly in or out of, the only difference between the simulator and its real counterpart is the panel of instruments to my left, which allow Sandy Howard, the "senior check" (supervising) captain of the day, to simulate any problem that could occur during a real flight. Today, he is using that panel of instruments to put Qantas Captain Ian Emery, First Officer Bruce Milne, and Flight Engineer Len Waddell through a series of recurrent training exercises. During my research for this book, I was allowed to sit in and watch to see how they handled those problems.

The "Senior Check" Captain They Love to Hate!

With a flick of a switch or two, Howard can make life pretty miserable for these guys. They can be roaring down the runway and right at Velocity-1—or V-1, the decision speed at which point the captain must make a split-second decision to take off or do a "rejected takeoff," or RTO—and Howard will turn to the panel and make an engine explode. Or as Captain Emery has the jet in a climb, Howard will reach over and make the instruments that tell him his "attitude"—the jet's angle in relation to the horizon—fail. Or as Emery is coming in for a landing, Howard might reduce the pilot's instrument assistance to a minimum and make the visibility so poor that Emery can't see the ground until seconds before the plane touches down. Howard can even use the "magic panel" to produce wind shear conditions during a landing or takeoff.

In short, anything that can go wrong with a plane will go wrong at the most inconvenient times, here in the simulators where Qantas's crews are put through these exercises. (Sessions include briefing and debriefing periods before and after the time spent in the simulator.) If any officer doesn't perform satisfactorily, missing the mark when the exercise is discussed and attempted again, he or she will be grounded until the officer has polished his or her performance with further training sessions and a follow-up test.

Doing It by the Book

The exercise we've just done in "Hong Kong" is exercise number 128. The Qantas training program—which is based on Boeing's training and aircraft manual, incorporates Qantas's own requirements, and is approved by the Civil Aviation Authority in Australia—includes hundreds of procedures a crew might expect to cover over a three-year period, many more than once. That's not including in-flight spot checks that will take place.

After the handling of the engine failure while heading into "Hong Kong," the Qantas crew now must do the approach to Hong Kong after losing two engines—which in real life is extremely rare—the second failure occurring *after* the "go-around." Although the plane is missing two engines and their reverse thrust power routinely used to help slow down the landing plane on the runway, Milne finishes the landing safely by activating an extremely sophisticated and effective automatic braking system designed to prevent any of the wheels from skidding. He does not rely on the reverse thrust from the remaining two working engines because that force would alter the symmetry of power, possibly causing the plane to turn off the runway.

"Any failure is going to heighten your pulse rate a little," explains Ken Anderson, "senior check" flight engineer responsible for the initial and recurrent training of Qantas flight engineers, who is briefing me on the exercises today. "But we practice the maneuvers so many times that, if the real thing were to happen, we would not be in a state of shock but able to handle the problem quite proficiently." That, of course, is music to the ears of any recovering fearful flier. Watching the performance of the crew today, I have no problem believing Anderson.

Handling Rejected Takeoffs

Today's session seems to be focused on RTOs—rejected takeoffs—a perfect subject for me, as takeoff was always my particular bête noire and I'm several days away from a real flight from Sydney to Los Angeles. I'm intrigued to hear about V-1—the speed at which the "Go/No Go" decision is made, which varies with the plane's weight but is about 150 m.p.h. (240 k.p.m.) at medium weights—and V-2, the speed at which the plane climbs away from the runway, which is about

The Boeing 747-400 successfully performs one of the most critical tests conducted on new airplanes: the 100 percent maximum-energy refused takeoff. This test demonstrates to the Federal Aviation Administration that the airplane's brakes, in their most diminished state, can still stop a fully loaded plane if there is a need to abort a takeoff.

20 percent faster than V-1. The flight engineer on 747s looks out for malfunctions before the plane reaches V-1 and usually reports—or "calls" them, which is the word crew members use in this situation—and the takeoff can be rejected in time.

With malfunctions that happen on or after V-1 or decision point, the plane will still be allowed to take off. The malfunction will be "called" after the landing gear is up, the plane has reached an altitude of about 400 feet (120 meters), and the crucial part of the takeoff is over. (Engine failure or fires, however, are called regardless of the plane's position in the takeoff phase.) As the plane continues to climb, the crew checks all the other systems for satisfactory operation and then brings the plane back to land at the airport, if a return is required. Airport returns are required when proceeding to another airport would compromise the safe operation of the aircraft, such as in the case of an uncontrollable engine fire or a cargo door that is not closed completely.

The takeoff is allowed to continue in this case because most malfunctions after V-1—ranging from an engine fire or engine failure to a burst tire—do not impair a plane's ability to take off and fly. Rejecting a takeoff after V-1, on the other hand, is likely to cause the plane to overshoot the runway, possibly injuring passengers as well as the aircraft. Therefore, a malfunction has to be in the "catastrophic" category to merit an RTO after V-1. That would mean something like a failure of four engines—an extremely unlikely occurrence.

In today's session, the one point when a takeoff or RTO does not go smoothly is when Howard programs the plane to have a burst tire just *after* V-1, when the plane is at a high weight of about 350 tons (315 metric tons), and instructs the crew to make the incorrect choice of rejecting the takeoff anyway to demonstrate what will happen. We hear a loud bang amidst the roar of the engines, then feel a lot of jolting after the RTO. "Where are we?" I ask Ken Anderson, who's explaining these exercises in the simulator for me.

"We're creating a new freeway, basically," he quips, referring to the furrows we're presumably plowing with the plane's wheels past the end of the runway in a section of field used as an emergency stopping area. "It's a split-second decision at the time," Howard explains to me of the choice to be made at V-1. A burst tire could damage the exterior of the plane, because it could expel rapidly rotating hunks of thick rubber, but probably not affect the plane's ability to fly. We go through the exercise again, and this time Captain Emery continues the takeoff successfully.

Engine Failures

In the next exercise, a rapidly rising exhaust gas temperature (EGT) and stall cause engine number one to fail before V-1, and the takeoff is rejected. (A rising EGT usually is caused by damage in the combustion area of the engine or by the failure of the fuel flow regulation system.) Later, a similar problem after V-1 is dealt with by continuing the takeoff, reducing the thrust on the ailing engine to keep its temperature down, then returning to the airport. In this case, the crew will use the rudder of the plane to counteract any imbalance caused by the reduced thrust on one engine.

Next they practice handling high vibration in engine number one. "Up to eighty knots, the flight engineer watches the indicators on the panels and calls problems he or she sees," Anderson tells me. "After eighty knots, the flight engineer monitors the indicators and sees the warning lights but won't say anything. An EGT warning light, for example, tells us we are near the limit but requires no call—just close monitoring to make sure that there is no exceeding of the limit. We don't want to reject a takeoff for anything that is not a significant problem."

"If there's an engine failure at V-1, the plane will fly even at high weights," continues Anderson. "Even with a second engine failure, there's a good chance the plane will fly okay. If we lose three engines, we'd have to be at a *very* light weight to fly." In this case, adds Anderson, the crew would rapidly jettison fuel to lighten the plane's load, a rare but not dangerous procedure to discard up to about one third of the plane's total weight, or more than 220,000 pounds (99,000 kilograms) in a heavily laden aircraft. A plane can also be aided by the "ground effect," the compression of air close to ground or water that enables a plane—or a bird—to stay airborne with less effort. The molecules of air are "squeezed" between the aircraft and the earth or water because there is a positive pressure exerted beneath an aircraft.

Anderson reassures me that, if an engine explodes, modern engines can usually contain that explosion without any damage to the rest of the plane. Even if the captain has a heart attack—a favorite worst-case scenario for a lot of fearful fliers—first officers are trained to take over, with the help of the flight engineer. In fact, captains and first officers—both are pilots—often alternate sectors of a flight, so both have practice with dealing with malfunctions as well as with normal operating procedures. Malfunctions are not uncommon, but they certainly are not experienced at the level they are in the simulator, and passengers are not informed of them unless the scheduled operation of the plane is affected or if for some reason it involves the passengers directly.

Equipment Failures

Other exercises hone pilots' skills at handling instrument failure. We go through one impressive high-wire scenario where Captain Emery is in V-2, with the plane climbing away from the runway, when he spots a warning light telling him that his "attitude" indicator has failed.

To handle this problem, the captain asks the first officer what the indications are, Anderson explains. (The captain's instruments are repeated on the first officer's side.) Captain Emery also checks a centrally located "standby horizon indicator" and sees that this indicator agrees with what the first officer is telling him. The captain then transfers the first officer's information over to his side. This whole *pas de deux* takes place while the crew is simultaneously communicating with the air traffic control tower and retracting the jet's landing gear and its flaps on the leading and trailing edges of each wing, which change the wing shape to produce lift at low speeds.

At 3,000 feet (915 meters), the crew members swiftly run through their checklist to make sure, first of all, that they've done the correct procedure and, second, that nothing else is wrong with the plane. Fortunately, it's a checklist that most officers could recite in their sleep. "These checklists are extremely important and are committed to memory," Anderson informs me. "These are known as the 'memory items' of our 'non-normal procedures.'"

Later, a similar exercise is carried out whereby the first officer's compass fails, indicated by a warning light, as he's performing the takeoff in the captain's place. This time, it's the first officer who trades information with the captain. On a subsequent landing, Howard reduces both the instrument assistance and the visibility outside to a minimum to help the crew members hone their navigational skills. They must work together to calculate their height and the right rate of descent. This exercise goes smoothly, but I'm reassured to hear that, if the rate of descent is too rapid close to the ground, a computerized voice will call out, "Sink rate, sink rate! Pull up, pull up!" Likewise, if the landing gear is not down and locked at low altitude when the aircraft is configured for landing, a warning horn will go off that cannot be silenced until the problem is fixed.

A Panoply of Practice Exercises

I observe a variety of other exercises by the flight crew today. For example, First Officer Milne practices an instrument landing (following a radio beam) with a twenty-knot crosswind on the runway, which is indicated to him not only by the air traffic control tower but also by the jet's navigational system. Anderson tells me that the crews also practice taking off and landing with wind shear conditions; indeed, the conditions programmed in the simulator's computer are modeled on real conditions that have been experienced by pilots. "Sometimes they use emergency thrust to make sure the plane will fly," Anderson says of landings and takeoffs in wind shear. "It's a very interesting exercise."

Wind shear is a rapid change of direction or wind speed over a short distance, whether it's vertical or horizontal, and most turbulence experienced by aircraft is in fact a type of wind shear (see the chapter on weather, page 86, for more information). "If we're approaching any type of cloud, we prepare for it, particularly if we're close to storm clouds containing rain, wind, and occasionally hail," relates Anderson. "Turbulence can also be generated by land forms, so if we have a howling westerly wind in Sydney, there will likely be ongoing turbulence from the air masses moving through the mountains west of Sydney. This is sometimes called a 'standing wave.' It's like a reef that causes a surge."

Later, we take off from another airport for low-visibility training—simulators are programmed to move to any airport in the world in a matter of seconds. We take off in fog that hinders visibility beyond 200 meters (220 yards). "We use a higher thrust so we're on the ground a lesser amount of time," Anderson observes. "There's such low visibility that you want to be airborne quickly." This takeoff feels sharper than the others, but Anderson points out that the thrust is still only at 75 to 80 percent of maximum capability. "If we used maximum takeoff thrust at medium weight (265 tons or 238 metric tons), you'd feel as if you were in one of the new 737s that seem to take off almost vertically," he adds.

That's hard to imagine in our seemingly ponderous 747. Yet when I ask Anderson why it feels as if we're going slower in takeoff in the 747 than in the 737, he replies that the speeds are similar but that the larger size of the 747 gives the impression that it's moving slower. Another illusion is created when you are in a moving car near an airport, watching a plane land or take off: Often the plane appears to be nearly at a standstill. (That always worried me!)

During one of the last maneuvers of the day, the crew practices a low-visibility approach using the jet's autopilot. Anderson explains, to my surprise, that the workload on both pilots remains high in this situation, because they must constantly monitor the controls to make sure that everything is working properly. "You're always looking at the instruments, listening for warning calls, and checking on traffic," he says. "You never sit back and assume that everything is okay."

More music to my ears.

FEARFUL FLIER TO FREQUENT FLIER: RICHARD HARDWICK'S STORY

As a youth, it was much easier to travel than it is now. There seemed to be a factor of trust that fostered a feeling of being safe. That's been lost recently. Somehow in all the plastic nature of things these days and the way we travel, I lose a sense of humanity behind the whole thing. These planes are huge.

—Peter McGee
fearful flier, New Canaan, Connecticut

When I called Richard Hardwick to talk to him about his recovery from fear of flying, he had just returned from a business trip that had taken him from Sydney to London to Paris, back to London, and then on to Calcutta and Singapore before returning home—all in three weeks. This is a man who once suffered from a fear so debilitating that he was bedridden with depression before he conquered it.

I first heard Hardwick talking about overcoming fear of flying when I was visiting Sydney for the first time, in early 1992. Dreading the long flight back to Paris, where I was living then, I shared my own fears with him and was filled with admiration for this tough fellow who had tackled his fears head-on. When I was ready to do the same a few years later, Hardwick told me more about the course, which not only had helped him get on a plane but ultimately had enabled him to advance in his career to such an extent that he is now traveling around the world.

Early in his life, Hardwick had flown comfortably. His fears blossomed when he was in his late teens, drinking heavily and abusing drugs. It started with acrophobia—fear of heights—and agoraphobia—fear of open spaces—but it wasn't long before aviophobia was added to this crippling cocktail. Although he'd gotten clean and sober by the age of twenty-five, Hardwick was living in Australia and constantly coming up with excuses why he couldn't fly back to visit his family back in the United States. He hadn't been in any type of aircraft since the age of fifteen.

"I would look at a 747 flying through the air above me, and I couldn't believe the thing could fly," Hardwick tells me. "It was doing it right in front of my eyes, but I didn't believe that anything that big could fly at that angle, taking off. I always expected it to stall and drop to the ground. I was afraid of being up so high and not having control of the vehicle," he continues. "I didn't trust the environment, the plane, or the people operating it. Because I couldn't see them, it felt like a faceless experience. When you get on a bus, you can see the bus driver. When you get in a cab, you can see the cab driver. On a plane, you can't see the crew, just an enormous jet and little windows up front. It seemed to be that they weren't human."

Hardwick, now in his late thirties, began the process of gluing his psyche together after he quit alcohol and drugs in his mid-twenties. He didn't have to deal with the issue of flying for a while, because he was working in sales and marketing for a construction materials company, and there was no need to travel. At age thirty, however, he began working for the Sydney office of a multinational construction materials company and was completely responsible for developing its marketing to the mining industry. As his department's projects gained momentum, Hardwick started getting calls from prospective clients—mines and mining construction contractors—in other parts of Australia. That was the good news; the bad news was that they wanted him to be present for on-site technical assistance, which was another aspect of his job.

"That forced my hand. I was supposed to fly to Tasmania via Melbourne and pick up a colleague in Melbourne," Hardwick narrates. "I felt so much fear that for the three days prior to that flight I felt absolute terror. I felt an overwhelming dread of my impending death, I had the sensation of pins and needles through my fingers and arms, and my feet were cold. It seemed unreal. I was obsessed with this flight! I didn't sleep that night before and by the time the morning came, I was a mess. I didn't show up and catch the plane."

Hardwick's colleague thought he had missed the flight and called their boss. Hardwick called in sick, and he was sick indeed. "I felt I had failed. I went into a three-day bedridden depression," he admits. "This had never happened to me before and never has since. I couldn't even make a decision to turn over. It was then that I realized that I had to do something about my fear of flying."

When Hardwick came to the Fearless Flyers clinic, he learned for starters that the engines were not going to fall off the wings. " I mistrusted flying based on a total ignorance of the technical process," he says. "The course was brilliant. It made the whole experience very matter-of-fact, and more important, it showed how ordinary the pilots were. They weren't test pilots out to take risks, but down-to-earth, steady individuals. What helped more was learning that the pilots are tested on their academic and practical abilities in the simulators on a regular basis—and that they're not covered by any special life insurance policies!" Hardwick reports. "They're not like those people who put out oil fires: They have the same insurance as you and me." Perhaps the most helpful aspect of the course, though, was the lesson on the physics of flight. "I learned that, no matter what I believed about it, the plane would go up," he states. "It's a law of nature, and I can't change a law of nature."

That might have been the end of the story, except that Hardwick was lazy about doing the relaxation exercises suggested by the course. He believes this was why, during the one-hour graduation flight from Sydney to Melbourne, he suffered a severe panic attack, complete with dizziness, pins and needles, dry mouth, and all the trimmings. He couldn't even speak until Dr. Burke helped him out of the attack with relaxation exercises.

Undaunted, Hardwick took the eight-week course again. "The second time, I really paid attention. I practiced everything they told me to do—vigorously and without a moment's hesitation," he testifies. When it came time for his second graduation flight, Hardwick was armed with additional exercises a psychiatrist outside the clinic had given him to dissipate nervous energy in his limbs. When the plane was taking off, for example, he pedaled his feet as if running with the plane and moved his clenched fists forward in short, circular motions. He also listened constantly to Dr. Burke's instruction tape on deep breathing and relaxation and performed those exercises too.

The difference was dramatic. "When the plane took off, I experienced none of the unpleasant feelings I had felt before, and I couldn't believe it," he says. "I just kept doing the tape. I also used my knowledge of what they'd told me, such as the physics of flying." Taking another bit of advice from the course, Hardwick began to practice whenever he could, to this day armed on his flights with relaxation tapes and notes from the course. Joined by fellow Fearless Flyers graduates, he followed up the course with a series of weekend "mystery flights," in which the graduates would buy inexpensive tickets, unaware of their destination until they got on the plane. With several of those adventures under his belt, he began booking flights for business, and the world opened up for him.

Two promotions and more than 250 flights later, he has moved to Montreal, Quebec, to be his company's corporate market manager for mining. "The course has revolutionized my life," he affirms. "I've learned firsthand about cultures I'd only read about in books, and I've seen the historical places I've studied. I'm a real history nut, and traveling has enriched the tapestry of my life. I realized I've only got one life—you grab it by the throat and give it a shake!"

Overcoming his fear of flying has touched him on a more profound level as well. "It has made me realize my biggest defect of character was my fear and how much control it had over me," Hardwick says in more hushed tones. "To see fear like this diminish and dissolve gives me a sense of gratitude that is deep and exhilarating."

SIZE DOESN'T MATTER: WHY YOUR PLANE WILL STAY UP

The whole thing didn't make sense: How could this big, heavy thing stay in the air? I had visions of the plane plummeting to earth—that there'd be no second chance.

—Kathryn Bendall
Fearless Flyers class of November 1995

One night during my own Fearless Flyers stint, while we were sitting in a circle sharing what aspect of the course was helping us the most, one of the men in the class extolled the benefits of the course's education on aerodynamics. "Oh, to be a man!" wailed one of the women in the course. "Concentrate on the mechanics and forget the emotions!"

As hard as we laughed—and even if we agreed with her about differences between the sexes—none of us argued the fact that the lesson on aerodynamics had done us a world of good. Never mind that some of us hadn't understood some of the more technical explanations: We finally knew why planes stayed in the air and didn't think of a successful takeoff as a defiance of nature or a fluke.

"Some people feel that the bigger the airplane is, the less likely it is that it's going to fly," notes Ken Dunkley, the Qantas manager of mechanical systems engineering and licensed pilot who has taught Fearless Flyers classes since the early 1980s. "They have trouble understanding that the airplane flies independently of its size, and that the smallest airplane flies in exactly the same way as the biggest one. Big ones don't need to be totally different to fly just because they're bigger." In this chapter, Dunkley not only explains how a plane flies but also addresses aerodynamics questions that often concern fearful fliers, such as why the power is often cut back during a takeoff, why it's okay if a plane lands firmly, and why it's desirable for the wings to move.

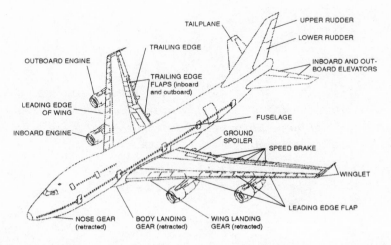

A diagram of a Boeing 747 and its major components

THE ENGINEER'S PERSPECTIVE, WITH KEN DUNKLEY

All airplanes fly on exactly the same principle—no matter how big or small. Flying depends on the shape of the wing, which if you look at it in a cross section, has a very elongated teardrop shape, more curvy on the top than on the bottom. As the air flies over the wing, because the aircraft is actually flying forward through the air, the pressure on top of the wing is reduced and the pressure on the bottom is increased. That's how you get the upward force that pushes the airplane up in the air and holds it up in the air.

As the plane is flying, it's balanced: The lift of the wing exactly equals the weight of the airplane. As I said, whether it's the smallest or largest airplane, or even a model airplane, the principle's exactly the same. You could build an airplane double the size of a 747—and it would still fly in exactly the same way. The biggest airplane flying today is a Russian military transport aircraft that is about 40 percent bigger than a 747.

Unlike a speedboat that runs over the top of the water, bouncing on the top of something, airplanes fly through something—the air. It's purely the shape of the wing that keeps the plane up. You can prove that to yourself if you get out a small, light piece of paper. Hold it upwards at its bottom corners, letting the paper fall over on the side away from you, and blow over the top of it. The paper will actually rise up because

*Boeing's 737, 747, and 767 models are
among the most popular jets used by airlines.*

the air pressure is reduced a little bit as it flows over the curved top surface of the paper.

In technical terms, this is caused by the effect described in
Bernoulli's principle, which says that the total pressure in the air remains
constant. Anything that moves has dynamic energy, also called
"dynamic pressure." Air is no different, and you feel this for yourself on
a windy day when the air blows against your house or your clothing,
and the faster the wind blows, the higher the pressure becomes. Air also
has static pressure, which we feel when we ascend a tall building very
rapidly in an elevator and our ears "pop." Bernoulli's principle says that

the sum of this dynamic pressure and the static pressure must remain the same. Think back to the wing again, which is more curvy on top than it is on the bottom. As the airplane flies through the air, the air passing over the curvy top of the wing has a bigger distance to travel so it speeds up. As it does, the dynamic pressure increases and the static pressure drops. The static pressure exerts a force at right angles to the direction of the flow, and this force "sucks" the wing upwards. On the bottom of the wing, a similar thing happens, but because the wing is flatter on the bottom, the air has a shorter distance to travel and actually slows down slightly. Slowing down, the air has lost some dynamic energy, so the static pressure goes up to keep the total pressure the same. This increase in static pressure results in an upward force on the bottom of the wing, pushing the airplane up. It is the total of this reduced pressure above the wing and increased pressure below the wing that applies an upward force equal to the airplane weight and lifts the airplane off the ground.

People often ask, "Why can't you make an airplane fly really slowly and take off at a really nice, slow speed that I feel comfortable with, and then rip across the Pacific Ocean super-fast so I can get to my holiday destination quickly?" It's not quite that easy. A wing that flies very slowly has lots of curvature and therefore lots of lift at low speeds, but is also very thick, so it can't push through the air all that easily. On the other hand, a skinny, thin wing will fly through the air very quickly, but it doesn't fly as well at low speeds. For this reason, you can't have an airplane that flies both slowly and quickly without adapting it in some special way, like adding flaps to the trailing edge of the wing that alter the curvature of the wing and make it fly more slowly.

The things that come out of the trailing edge of the wing and sometimes the leading edge of the wing when an airplane is landing or taking off are called "flaps." They increase the curvature of the wing to give the plane more lift at low speeds, but they also cause drag at high speed. When an aircraft takes off and is ready to speed, the flaps are slowly retracted until the wing is slim and streamlined, which allows the plane to fly very fast. When it's time to land, the flaps come out again, making the wing curvy again.

The Takeoff

When the aircraft is sitting on the ground, it's horizontal. The wings are not producing any lift, because the aircraft is standing still. As the aircraft accelerates down the runway, however, the air flows over the wings with more force. When the plane reaches a certain speed, the pilot pulls the control column back and pitches the nose up, so that the wing is

A Boeing 757 commences its takeoff from the runway.

presented to the air at a slightly nose-up angle. The wing starts to develop lift, and soon lifts the airplane off the ground.

Meanwhile, the pilot balances the lift generated by the passage of the wings through the air against the downward pull of the weight of the plane. To climb, the pilot raises the nose a little, the wing produces more lift, and the aircraft climbs to its cruising altitude. When the plane gets there, the pilot puts the nose down a little, reducing the lift so that the aircraft doesn't continue to climb and can fly horizontally. It sounds difficult—how do you juggle a lifting force so that it exactly balances a weight that you obviously can't measure?—but it's quite easy and natural when you're flying an airplane. It's like steering a car straight.

Power Reductions During Climbs

During the takeoff roll and initial climb, the engines are producing full power, but after that initial climb, there is no point in using maximum power if less power will still allow the aircraft to climb safely. Reducing the thrust decreases the wear on the engines, helping to prolong their life spans. Of course, the pilot always has control of the engines and can increase thrust at any time if, for example, air traffic control asks him or her to climb to a higher altitude or fly a little faster.

Another reason for the engines to be cut back is noise abatement. In order to cut down the noise in certain areas, such as residential neighborhoods, the pilot may initially climb fairly steeply and then climb less steeply once the plane has reached the noise-sensitive areas. Another way to reduce noise in certain areas is to require the plane to turn just after takeoff and fly on a different route.

A Boeing 767 banks left over water.

Turning the Plane

Apart from simply moving forward, an aircraft can move in three other ways. It can ascend and descend; it can turn left or right—this is called "yawing"—or it can roll to make the left wing go up or the right wing go up, which is called "banking." Some people worry when the aircraft banks to make a turn, but it is no different than leaning when you ride a bicycle around a corner. These three directions are guided by the control column and the rudder pedals. When the control column is moved back or forward, it makes the aircraft go up or down. When the pilot turns a wheel on the control column, the aircraft banks left or right. The pilot also has his or her feet on the rudder pedals, and these make the nose move left or right to yaw the aircraft. All three columns are used simultaneously to keep the aircraft in balance in level flight or in a turn.

That may sound difficult. If you're driving a car, all you have to do is steer it and make it go fast or slow, while in an airplane, you simultaneously use three controls to make it go up and down and left and right, and make it roll. When you try it, it's actually quite easy.

The Landing

When the aircraft is descending to land, the pilot reduces the thrust of the engine so that the aircraft starts to fly more slowly. Likewise, the lift of the wing is reduced and the aircraft starts to descend. The pilot flies down a precisely controlled path produced by a radio beam, called the "glide slope." This beam tells the pilot if the plane is too high, too low, or just right, with information displayed on the instruments in the cockpit. At some airports, a visual light system also guides the pilot. During the descent, the pilot keeps the aircraft aligned with the center line of the runway and monitors the flight speed. When the plane reaches the end of the runway, the pilot reduces the thrust on the engine and pulls back on the nose to get the aircraft into a more horizontal position. The pilot lands the main wheels—the ones that are about halfway along the body of the plane—on the runway, then gently lowers the nose using elevators that control the pitch of the airplane. Overall, landing is a little more tricky than takeoff.

Passengers shouldn't worry if the aircraft appears not to touch down with a feather-light touch, because the aircraft has to be converted from a rapidly flying machine into a relatively slow wheelborne machine very quickly. It's the brakes that stop the aircraft, so the lift on the wing should be destroyed quickly so that the aircraft can settle on its wheels and the brakes can take effect and slow the airplane down. Some people think, "That was a terrible landing—we landed so firmly," but in fact it may not have been a terrible landing. Moreover, the aircraft is designed by the manufacturer to absorb the landing impact. It's terrible feeling the airplane landing on the ground with a thump and thinking it's going to break, but it can take far greater loads than that without breaking.

Roaring into Reverse Thrust

To be safe and to give the plane some extra security during the landing, the aircraft uses reverse thrust, a process in which the engine produces a thrust in the opposite direction. It doesn't mean the engine goes backwards—rather, the power of the engine is deflected, so that the air that normally comes straight out of the back of the engine is projected forward, producing "reverse thrust." If you're sitting in the cabin of the aircraft, the airplane is coming down nicely, gliding toward the runway, touching down, and suddenly the engines make a lot of noise—it's just the engines giving you extra stopping power with reverse thrust. Even without the reverse thrust, though, the aircraft would still have stopped.

No "Winging It"

Each takeoff and landing on a 747 or any other aircraft is a precisely calculated mathematical operation. The pilot does not run down the runway and say, "Well, I think we're going fast enough now."

The speed at which an aircraft will take off depends on its weight. We know exactly how much each airplane weighs because we weigh them every so often, and we know how much fuel we put on, the weight of passengers, the weight of bags and the special freight. From that, and from the research the manufacturer has done, we know the speed at which the aircraft will fly. But we take off at an even higher speed than that, just to be safe. We consider the length of the runway, the temperature outside, the speed of the wind over the runway, and the speed at which the aircraft will fly safely. With all this information, the pilots and the copilot monitor the speed as the aircraft runs down the runway until the plane reaches the speed it needs to safely fly, then the aircraft takes off and flies away.

Likewise with the landing, we know the weight the aircraft is going to be when landing because we knew how much it was when it took off, and we know how much fuel it has burned. Pilots can work out the runway distance necessary to land from tables provided by the manufacturer, ensuring that the runway is long enough and that aircraft can be stopped using the brakes on the wheels alone.

Avoiding Stalls

There is a minimum speed at which an aircraft can fly, called the "stall speed." An airplane can get to a point where it can't fly any more slowly, because the airflow over the wing breaks up, and the aircraft loses its lift and stalls. If it does, the aircraft will drop fairly quickly while the pilot regains control. In regular passenger service, pilots make sure the speed of the plane is well above the minimum safe speed, so passengers will never feel what it is like to be in an aircraft "at the stall." The only way you are ever going to experience a stall is to go to a training field and ask a flying instructor to take you for a ride in a training aircraft.

When an aircraft is about to stall, the controls will alert the pilot of the impending stall well before the plane has reached stalling speed. The air flowing off the wing becomes turbulent, striking the tail plane so the aircraft vibrates. As the plane vibrates, it becomes physically difficult to pull the control column back to make the nose pitch higher. If the plane did approach stall conditions, the pilot could either lower the nose a little and start to descend or put more power in the engine and fly faster, and the plane wouldn't stall. Apart from the physical characteristics of a stall, modern aircraft have various electronic devices to alert the pilot well before a stall condition.

Now, some people confuse the action of speed brakes with stalls. Speed brakes are on top of the wings and allow the aircraft to descend more quickly. Unlike a car, an airplane does not have brakes for slowing down in the air, except for the speed brakes on the wing. Flat panels that come out of the top of the wing, speed brakes slow the airplane down by creating drag. In doing so, they often create turbulence that will hit the tail plane. If you're in a descending aircraft, and you start to feel as if the plane is going over a bumpy road, it's not that the aircraft's stalling. It's the speed brakes slowing the aircraft down, perhaps because

Among the precertification tests performed on Boeing jets (the 777 is pictured here) are VMUs—velocity minimum unsticks—which are used to determine the airplane's minimum takeoff speed. The test requires the airplane's protected tail (close-up) to come in contact with the runway prior to takeoff. Sensors on the tail indicate the distance from the ground. Boeing incorporates this data into flight manuals used by the airlines.

air traffic control has asked the plane to slow down because there's another airplane in front of it.

Steeper Climbing

Two-engine airplanes climb more steeply than four-engine airplanes. This is because part of the calculation of the takeoff assumes that, at the very worst possible time, one engine will fail. If one engine on a two-engine plane fails, there's one engine left, and the aircraft must have enough power to continue to take off safely and climb with only one engine. With two engines working, the airplane has twice as much thrust as it needs. A 747 or any four-engine airplane has four engines. Even if an engine failed at the most inconvenient time, there would still be three, so the aircraft would continue to climb. But the percentage of power lost is only 25 percent, as opposed to 50 percent, so the aircraft isn't as overpowered as a two-engine airplane. That's why two-engine airplanes generally climb quite steeply and four-engine airplanes not as steeply. Rest assured that if an engine failed on a four-engine airplane, it would still climb, easily exceeding any limits set down by the regulatory authorities.

During tests performed on the Boeing 777, computer stations set up in the jet's interior gather data from all over the aircraft.

Endurance Testing

Manufacturers such as Boeing subject airplanes to dreadful things in tests before they let them go into passenger service. They load them up with huge amounts of weight in the form of barrels of water or bags of sand, making sure that they can fly with a weight far higher than what it would be for normal service. And they load the tail of the airplane up with heavy objects such as bags of lead to make sure it can fly with all the weight in the back, at the front, or at one side. Next, they test the landings. Instead of letting the airplane touch down moderately and gently, they just drive it straight into the runway with a great thump and see what happens. Then they go down the runway at the fastest possible speed while keeping the airplane on the ground, then stomp on the brakes as hard as they can, to see what happens to the wheels and the brakes.

Those tests ensure that, in normal passenger service where it won't get anywhere near these kinds of conditions, the plane will be fully controllable and safe to fly. Some of the tests are quite spectacular to see. When Boeing tested its 747-400 to make sure it would still take off successfully if they dragged the tail on the ground, it still took off and flew.

Flexing Wings

The wing—I say "wing" because it actually is one solid piece—is designed to be flexible. If it were rigid, aircraft couldn't fly through

The wings of a Boeing 777 were pulled twenty-four feet above their normal position before they broke during a full-scale destruct test performed at the Boeing Commercial Airplane Group's plant in Everett, Washington. Computer-controlled hydraulic actuators applied about a half a million pounds of pressure on each wing—the equivalent weight of a fully-loaded 777—until both wings broke simultaneously at the predicted position. The test confirmed that the airplane's wings exceeded their maximum design requirement, which is one-and-a-half times the loads experienced in the most extreme flight conditions.

bumps and turbulence nearly as smoothly as they do. The wing flexes up and down, movement that you can see when you look out the window. It's like springs in your car—if you didn't have them you'd feel every little bump along the road. The wings are like a huge spring that spreads out the movement of the air, giving the body of the plane a relatively smooth ride. The wing, being a flexible thing, bends up as the aircraft flies. The wing is capable of bending down but never does because the aircraft would have to fly upside down to get the load in the other direction.

Sometimes when passengers look out of the windows, they see what looks like trails of fuel or smoke. This vapor is actually what are called "vortices"—you can see moisture condensing from the air. The wing has high-pressure air underneath and low-pressure air above, and the air flows around the tip of the wing to equalize the pressure. As it flows around the tip, vortices, like horizontal cyclones or tornadoes, come off the wing. These vortices are visible when the plane flies through moist air. Sometimes, with aircraft such as the 767, you can see a magnificent vortex going over the wing at takeoff if you're sitting close to the leading edge of the wing.

Door Security

Fearful fliers sometimes ask, "What if a deranged person opened the door in flight and did something terrible?" The simple answer is that this is impossible because the doors are actually plugs. That sounds strange when you look at a 747, where the door is on the outside of the airplane when the aircraft is on the ground. But as it goes into the fuselage, the central structure of the airplane, it goes through a very clever little motion: The door is tapered like a sink plug, and the aircraft fuselage is tapered like the sink, so you can't push the plug down through the sink, and neither can you push the door, once it's inside, back out through the hole of the fuselage. Pressurization holds it in the doorway. The handle is inside, but no person is strong enough to open the door against the pressurization load. You physically can't do it.

The aircraft is pressurized in flight because it flies more efficiently at higher altitudes. Not only that, it also has to fly over mountains. Of course it's uncomfortable for humans to be at 30,000 feet (9,146 meters)—we can't live at 30,000 feet, so the aircraft cabin is pressurized to simulate an altitude of about 6,000 to 7,000 feet (1,829 to 2,134 meters), a comfortable and safe altitude for us. This pressure differential between the inside of the airplane and the outside of the airplane is what holds the door in the doorway.

Some aircraft, such as the 767, have a door that slides up to the ceiling, so it doesn't move outside the fuselage. It just comes down out of the ceiling and moves outwards into the hole. Again, however, the door is tapered on the side like a plug. Once the door goes in, you can't push it out through the hole because pressurization holds it in place. When the aircraft lands, the pressure in the aircraft is equalized with the pressure outside the aircraft, so there's no differential pressure on the airplane. This makes it quite easy to open the door, because there's nothing holding it in the doorway.

Strength of Windows

Aircraft are mostly made of aluminum alloy, with steel in some areas that carry high loads, such as the landing gear. The passenger windows are not glass like those in a house, but rather a plastic material called "acrylic," which is flexible and not brittle. If you look closely at a passenger window on a Boeing aircraft, you will see it is actually made up of three separate layers. The outer layer is flush with the outside skin and retains the pressurization in the aircraft, acting as a structural member holding the air inside the aircraft. Inside this is an identically structured window that is not carrying any load, acting as a "backup window" that can carry the pressurization load in the unlikely case that the outer window develops a problem. The innermost window, the one you can actually touch, is there to protect the other two.

The 747 has a large, curved windscreen at the front, then a small triangle-shaped window, then a side window on each side of the cockpit. These windows are about one and a quarter inches thick and are made out of glass and acrylic. Acrylic's not very scratch-resistant, so a lot of the windows have a scratch-resistant layer of glass on the face, and the structural membrane in the middle is acrylic. It depends on the manufacturer. Between the two layers of glass or acrylic, there's an extremely thin layer of gold. It is deposited by a special process that can leave a layer so thin that we can see through it. Because gold is an exceptionally good conductor of electricity, an electrical current can still be passed through it to keep it warm and pliable, so the window won't shatter if the aircraft strikes a bird. This window is expensive—about US $4,838 (AUS $7,402).

The Thickness of the Skin

The thickness of the skin of a plane depends on the part of the airplane. Thicker parts near the root of the wing and the fuselage are about 0.4 inch thick and are made up of several layers of metal. The metal around doors and the landing gear is even thicker than that. The skin is generally made up of triple layers of metal plus a fitting of some sort on the inside—a forging or a casting. And between frames around the windows where it's not quite a structural member, it's about .08 inch thick. It's all aluminum alloy. There are some fiberglass parts in the nonstructural areas underneath the fuselage, which are just coverings over things, about an inch and a half thick, with a honeycomb structure. The parts of the airplane that carry the biggest loads, such as the landing gear and the engine mounting, are made of steel.

The Function of Winglets

The aircraft flies because it has higher pressure underneath the wing and lower pressure on top of the wing. At the tip of the wing, the air wants to flow from the high-pressure area underneath the wing to the low-pressure area above the wing, a process that can work against the force of the lift. What is ideal is to keep all that nice high pressure air under the wing, and all the low-pressure air on top of the wing, so that the two don't ever meet.

But of course, nature wants to equalize everything, so the air tends to flow around the wingtip. The winglet, the turned-up tip of the wings, combats this airflow around the wing. The improved understanding of airflow in the last few years has allowed the development of an effective winglet, and these are an easily recognizable feature of the 747-400, the latest model of the 747 aircraft. The winglet is cleverly designed to produce a vortex in the opposite direction to the vortex from the wing itself. This prevents the loss of lift by causing the air to spill up from the bottom of the wings, making the wing more effective because more high-pressure air is retained under the wing.

FLEXING THOSE WHITE KNUCKLES: KAREN TOMLINSON'S STORY

I had a bad experience many years ago with hitting an air pocket over the Catskills. That triggered dreams where I felt that I was falling in a downward-spiraling cyclic funnel.

—Peter McGee
fearful flier, New Canaan, Connecticut

Karen Tomlinson used to be the type of fearful flier who clutched the armrests of her seat as if, by doing so, she could hold the plane up all by herself. "I never ate on an airplane or even got out of my seat to go to the toilet," she recalls. "I was sick with terror."

When I met Tomlinson, an outgoing professional and mother of two from the Warrawee suburb of Sydney, she was standing in front of my class of fearful fliers, telling us not only how she had recovered from her phobia in this clinic but also how she had gone on to get her student pilot's license. As I sat in that class the first night, feeling jittery, I thought that someone who could now fly a plane by herself surely could not have been as badly afflicted as me, but Tomlinson had been. In fact, she was worse.

The phobia began when Tomlinson, now forty, was in her early twenties, taking a flight on a small turboprop plane from Port Moresby to Rabaul in New Guinea. The turbulence was so bad that "the plane was bobbing around the sky like a cork in the middle of a big ocean," Tomlinson recounts. "We were all terrified. I thought we were going to be killed—I thought the plane was going to break up or be thrown into a mountain." What should have been a transitory terror became for Tomlinson a deep-seated, irrational fear that resurfaced every time she flew. "From then on, I expected the same things to happen on every flight," she relates. "It didn't matter if the flight was as smooth as silk."

Tomlinson did anything to avoid flying, but sometimes had to because of her husband's work as a vascular surgeon, which periodically took him to England from their home in Sydney. Like so many other fearful fliers who still must fly, she developed superstitions and odd behavior when preparing for a trip. "If we had to fly, I did all the bookings, and I'd pick the date," she says. "It wouldn't matter how inconvenient the date was, I would not change it. That was one of my things. I felt that the flight I was going on was fate. With every crash I'd hear about, I would always think, 'Oh, those poor people! I wonder if any of them changed their flight to be on that one?'"

Tomlinson now believes that this constant state of anxiety took years off her life. "I didn't ever relax, even on a twenty-four-hour flight from Sydney to London without a single ripple along the way," she says. "I worried about everything—whether the fuel was contaminated, whether the cargo doors were closed properly, whether the pilot had had a good night's sleep or had an argument with his wife, whether the structure of the aircraft was strong enough to withstand any turbulence we might go through. After all that anxiety, I'd get to the other end and be totally exhausted. It took me twice as long as any normal person to get over the jet lag."

This went on for thirteen years before Tomlinson started thinking about doing something about it. She knew her fear wasn't rational: Her brother, a pilot for Qantas, had spent many hours explaining how the plane worked and how safe flight really was. Ultimately, however, "my fear of flying wasn't something I could get over myself," she concedes.

What prompted Tomlinson to get help was not only the fear itself but what it was doing to her life and her family. "I was turning down opportunities to go places because I didn't want to fly," she remembers. "I adore Europe, yet I kept saying, 'No, no, no!' because I couldn't face the twenty-four hours of flying necessary to get there. And even when I would go, I would spend far too much time thinking about getting back again. I wanted to go places and do things," Tomlinson continues. "It wasn't only me missing out—my children were too, and that was unfair. I was constantly saying they couldn't go here and couldn't go there because I had a problem! It was absurd. I desperately wanted to start going places and taking them with me."

In 1993, fate had it that Tomlinson was on a Qantas flight to London that her old friend, Paul Blanch, was crewing as a flight engineer. Blanch is one of the Qantas employees who has volunteered his time over the years to help demystify aviation for the fearful fliers who come to the Fearless Flyers clinic, even joining students on graduation flights. So, when Blanch saw how nervous his friend was when she was on the 747 to London that day, he talked her into taking the course.

I asked Tomlinson if there was a turning point for her in the course, and she said that the talk by Steve Symonds of the Bureau of Meteorology helped her the most, because turbulence was her personal demon. "Steve explained so well what turbulence is, what causes it, and what effect it has on aircraft," she says.

"The other important thing for me was the support of a group of people all in the same boat," Tomlinson explains. "When you have this kind of fear of something, it's very isolating." The graduation flight at the end of the course was for Tomlinson "the beginning of replacing every bad thought I had ever had about flying with happy, positive ones." In fact, when she was a volunteer during my own graduation flight, she told me, "Fly as often as you can. Each time it will get better, until one day you'll find you're looking forward to it."

For Tomlinson, it went even beyond coming to like flying. Once her attitude about piloting a plane had been like a fascination with sharks—"They're magnificent to watch, but you wouldn't want to go anywhere near one"—then she found herself considering taking flying lessons. "The clinic made such an enormous difference in my life," she explains. "When you conquer a major fear like that, it gives you confidence to do the other things you were reluctant to do. I thought learning to fly would be great fun." At the moment, Tomlinson doesn't aspire to aerobatics or in fact even anything beyond spending an hour at the controls with a flying instructor. "As a pilot, you are in control, but it's an exhilarating feeling of freedom," she describes. "It's wonderful. Now, when I think about the days when I was afraid of flying, that time seems like a different lifetime."

STORMY WEATHER: BUCKLE UP, NOT UNDER

The plane was bobbing around the sky like a cork in the middle of a big ocean. We were all terrified. I thought we were going to be killed— I thought the plane was going to break up or be thrown into a mountain. From then on, I expected the same things to happen on every flight. It didn't matter if the flight was as smooth as silk.

—Karen Tomlinson
Fearless Flyers class of May 1993

I t's remarkable how many people — even friends of mine who generally are not reluctant to fly—will stiffen in fright at the first sign of turbulence, sure that the plane could be knocked out of the sky at any moment. I love telling them that as long as they keep their seat belts fastened, inclement weather won't bring them any harm. The first thing you need to do at the mere suggestion of peaks and plunges on an airplane (*after* making sure you're buckled in!) is to forget the expression "air pocket." There is no such thing, just as water could not suddenly disappear in a spot under the bow of a ship at sea. Even when the plane drops, it is because it is being pushed by a downdraft. It is always flying, not falling.

It also helps to remember that planes are built to withstand far more abuse than they're going to get during any commercial flight, even if they get struck by lightning, and that your pilot is trained to avoid or to handle conditions such as thunderstorms, wind shear, and fog, with the help of a lot of sophisticated equipment. This is not to suggest that you should enjoy a bumpy flight the way you might enjoy a ride at an amusement park, but knowing what's going on can help you feel safe. Steve Symonds of the Australian Bureau of Meteorology in Sydney, who has been lecturing at Fearless Flyers clinics since 1979, aims to make weather events fascinating instead of frightening. Here, he explains the forms of weather that pilots look out for and why you won't be in danger if — here comes that maxim again — you *"keep your seat belt fastened!"*

THE METEOROLOGIST'S PERSPECTIVE, WITH STEVE SYMONDS

Pilots receive forecasts from the Bureau of Meteorology that tell them the weather at the place they're departing from and what the weather is likely to be along the way and at their destination. An important part of this route forecast is the prediction of the wind direction and wind speed at various levels in the atmosphere, key factors used in flight planning. If a flight can get a tailwind, it saves a lot of fuel, but if the plane will be battling a headwind, it's going to take longer to get to the destination. These forecasts of winds help pilots work out the best routes for their flights.

Today, flight planning for what we call "regular public transport" aircraft is done by computer. A central computer (in Australia, it's run by the Bureau of Meteorology) sends the wind forecast to the airline's computer, which then works out the best track for the flight. The pilots follow the route planned for them by this computer. Meteorologists also provide other information about the weather, such as the likelihood of thunderstorms and areas where turbulence, particularly clear air turbulence, is likely to occur.

What Causes Turbulence

The key concept in understanding turbulence is that, although you can't see it, air is a fluid and is constantly moving in all directions. When it blows past you and you're standing on the ground and can feel it, we call it wind. We know that the air is moving because we can feel the wind. But air doesn't only move in horizontal directions: It moves up and down, in diagonals, forward and back, and so on. Air moves in three dimensions and is constantly shifting.

When we take the ferry across Sydney Harbor, we're traveling over another fluid, which is the water in the harbor. We see the movement of the waves in the water, and we expect the ferry to go up and down as it goes over the waves. People expect the ferry to rock because they can see the waves, but people don't expect an aircraft to rock because they can't see the movement of the air.

Turbulence is the chaotic movement of the air. An aircraft flying through turbulent air is pushed away from its intended path. Rising air pushes the plane upwards, and descending air pushes it downwards. The plane can also be moved by headwinds, tailwinds, and winds from the side. Small changes to the flight path can be rectified quickly by the pilot, and the aircraft returns to its intended track.

Slight turbulence, the annoying small bumps or judders, is sometimes called "cobblestone turbulence" because it feels like riding a bicycle over a cobblestone road. Moderate turbulence causes difficulty for anyone walking round the cabin, while severe turbulence is the full roller-coaster ride. Think of it: In amusement parks around the world, people pay for the experience that you are getting free with your airline boarding pass.

When a mountain range rises out of the plains and wind blows across the plains toward the mountains, it can't go through them. It has to go over, so the air rises on one side of the range and descends on the other. When pilots started flying over mountain ranges — early flights didn't go very high and most were over water — they would feel sudden pushes upwards when they hit the rising air, and then, when they came over the other side, they hit the descending air. That's when the planes seemed to fall out of the sky, and people began calling these things "air pockets."

There's no such thing as an air pocket! You can't suddenly take the air away from underneath an airplane so that it falls down. The airplane will continue flying, even though the air is descending and pushing the plane downwards. Although a plane might be in turbulence, it is always flying — it's just being pushed around by the air, the same as the ferryboat is being pushed around by the water. When you're flying over mountains, relatively close to the ground, you can expect turbulence; the stronger the wind coming over the mountains, the greater the likelihood of turbulence. When you are flying over mountains, the pilot will put the "Fasten Seat Belts" light on, the cabin crew will sit down, and the plane is likely to bump around.

Similarly, if a plane is flying through clouds where you have very strong up-down drafts within the clouds themselves, the seat belt light will come on. As you sit there, you can often feel which way the wind is blowing the airplane, whether it's blowing it upwards, downwards, or sideways. If the change is sudden, you may feel as if you're on a roller coaster and have left your stomach behind. It's uncomfortable, but turbulence is to be expected in the up- and downdrafts inside these clouds.

What Is Meant by "Wind Shear"

"Wind shear" is a term we hear a lot, and it is often used by people who have no idea what it is. Wind shear is the rapid change in the direction or the speed of wind over a short distance.

This rapid change of wind speed or direction can produce the turbulent air. Wind shears can be produced by air blowing over hills and mountains, by jet streams, and by the up- and downdrafts in clouds, particularly thunderstorm clouds. When these shears are in the vertical plane—that is, an updraft close to a downdraft—waves very similar to those seen on a beach can be set up. These waves break and produce the chaotic air we call turbulence.

Wind shears also occur in microbursts, which we will look at later on page 90. These can be dangerous when the aircraft is close to the ground, although modern pilots are trained to avoid microbursts.

Clear Air Turbulence

The most frightening type of turbulence is clear air turbulence. This is when you're flying at high altitudes on a smooth, level flight with not a cloud in the sky, when all of a sudden, bang, bang, bang, the plane's all over the sky. Clear air turbulence does worry people. We have reports of it every now and again—there was an incident in early 1997 in which a plane hit some turbulence just south of Sydney, and people were injured on the flight. Interestingly, the people who were injured were mainly the flight attendants, not the passengers, and the reason for this was that the passengers had their seat belts on, but the flight attendants were walking around the cabin. People who get injured in turbulence accidents are not wearing their seat belts.

Clear air turbulence is associated with jet streams. Jet streams are fast-flowing rivers of air in the upper part of the troposphere—the lowest level of the atmosphere in which all weather and clouds are found—that generally flow from west to east in the middle latitudes. East-to-west-flowing jet streams are found near the equator and the poles. Jet streams can be hundreds of kilometers long and 31 to 63 miles (50 to 100 kilometers) wide—and the wind speeds in the center of them can be up to 250 miles (400 kilometers) per hour, although usually they are not quite that strong. Now that's a very, very strong current of air! I won't go into the technical details of the causes of jet streams; the simple explanation is that they are caused by horizontal temperature differences at high altitude levels. If you're flying from Perth to Sydney or from Los Angeles to New York, and you fly straight down the middle of the jet stream with a 250 m.p.h. tailwind, you'll get to your destination in no time at all. If you are trying to fly the other way, on the other hand, the last place you want to be is flying against a headwind like that, so pilots will fly around the jet stream to avoid that problem.

A jet stream is like a very fast-flowing river. In the center of a river, there is a smooth, fast-flowing core. Toward the edge, there are little whirlpools and eddies, a result of the friction between the water and the banks and the fact that the water flows faster in the middle than at the edges. The same thing happens in the upper atmosphere. There is a fast-flowing core of air, and whirlpools and eddies appear at the edges, often resembling breaking waves. If you hit one of these, the wind changes direction very suddenly, and the aircraft will be pushed around.

The air in a jet stream does not always flow in a straight line—it also spirals around the jet stream core. There is rising air on one side of the jet stream and descending air on the other. This can move the aircraft up and down, and the movement can be felt by passengers. The real turbulence, however comes from waves in the atmosphere, produced by wind shears, which break like those on a beach.

Injury from clear air turbulence is rare. In Australia, for example, there is a lot of light to moderate turbulence but only an average of one or maybe two occasions of severe turbulence per year. When you think of the number of flights in Australia in that time, you realize how rare it is that a plane hits turbulence so severe and unexpected that people are injured.

Withstanding Turbulence

As meteorologists, we do warn pilots of areas where turbulence is likely to occur. We learn where the jet streams are by putting balloons up and measuring the winds. We also get information from satellites and from other airplanes as well, and we plot these data on the charts we give to the pilots before the flight. When entering an area where turbulence is expected to occur, the pilot throttles back to a slower speed that is called "turbulence penetration speed." It's like driving a car over speed bumps: If you slow down, you hardly notice the bump, but if you stay at your normal speed, you get a terrible jolt. The same thing happens to airplanes: Slowing down makes the turbulence less of a jolt.

The thing to remember about turbulence is that aircraft are designed to withstand it. They are made to fly in any conditions that the atmosphere can present, and they are very, very strong machines. The airframe can take far more punishment than the pilots can, and pilots can take far more punishment than the passengers can. Pilots have experienced more turbulence than passengers and understand what it is, so the concern of pilots in turbulence is for the comfort of the passengers. Although the plane might be bouncing around all over the sky, the aircraft is safe. The pilots and the computers that are flying modern aircraft are looking after it.

The first thing you should do when you get on an airplane is fasten your seat belt. Whenever you're sitting in your seat, leave the seat belt fastened. If you hit turbulence and you've got your dinner or a drink in front of you, it might fly around, and your dinner might be upended onto your lap, but you're going to be okay, and you're not going to bounce around the cabin—as long as you're strapped in with the seat belt. That's why it's there. In fact, fewer people might be injured each year if attendants changed the spiel they give at the start of each flight to say, "Please wear your seat belt at all times when sitting down because if we hit turbulence, your seat belt will prevent you from bouncing off the ceiling."

Obviously, on a long flight you can't sit for thirteen or fourteen hours without moving. You should get up, have a walk around the cabin, stretch your legs, and go to the toilet. If the pilot is flying into an area where turbulence is expected, then she or he will usually put on the seat belt sign and make a little announcement, saying, "It's possible we could hit some turbulence in the next half hour, so I would advise people sitting in their seats to keep their seat belts fastened." When that happens, if you are wandering around, go back to your seat and put your seat belt on until the seat belt sign goes off again.

In the United States, flights tend to be bumpier than they are in Australia, because the mountains are higher: If you're flying from Los Angeles eastward, for example, there's no way to avoid the ranges. Learn to expect turbulence over mountain ranges—it's quite safe. Planes are designed to cope with turbulence, and the pilots know what they're doing. If you are in a plane that hits some turbulence and you're next to someone who's a little "green around the gills," share your knowledge with him or her. If you are near a window and can see the wings, have a look at them. You will notice that they are flexing up and down. The wings are designed to bend and absorb much of the turbulence. Wingtips of large aircraft can move twenty feet (six meters) or more, up or down, without the wing being damaged.

Avoiding Thunderstorms

Things that have caused problems in the past are large cumulus and cumulonimbus clouds, the clouds that create thunderstorms. A thunderstorm is a weather factory. It's an enormous cloud that goes from just above the ground right up to the stratosphere, and it has updrafts, downdrafts, hail, lightning, thunder, very strong winds near the ground, heavy rain, and on certain occasions, tornadoes. It's a nasty piece of work, indeed.

The weather radar is located in the front of any jet aircraft in the nose cone. Its beam goes side to side, covering a wide area in front of the aircraft and reflecting off the raindrops, snowflakes, and hailstones. It shows the pilot exactly where the storms are, so that the pilot can go around them. Pilots don't like flying through thunderstorms.

The 1997 flight in Australia (in which the flight attendants were injured in turbulence) was flying between two thunderstorm cells. The pilots could see the thunderstorm cells on the radar, but the area of turbulence extended out from the center of the storm, and that's what they hit. It wasn't as bad as it could have been—in fact, if they'd flown through the thunderstorm, the turbulence would have been a lot worse. I've flown around the edge of thunderstorms on a couple of occasions, and the plane was bouncing all over the sky—it was quite fun! It really helps to understand what's causing it. You also need to remember that turbulence in itself is not dangerous, because aircraft can withstand very severe turbulence. Turbulence can be dangerous when the aircraft is close to the ground and there is a violent change in wind direction or speed such as in a microburst.

Evading Microbursts

Large cumulus clouds and thunderstorm clouds have a hazard associated with them called the "microburst." As I said earlier, a thunderstorm cloud, or cumulonimbus cloud, is a weather factory. A lot of the fuel for the process of cloud development is latent heat. As cloud droplets condense from the water vapor, latent heat is given off. Latent heat is the extra heat required to change the state of water from a solid (ice) to a liquid (water) to a gas (water vapor). The heat required comes from the surrounding environment. For instance, if you lick your finger and hold it up to the wind, the finger feels cold on the windward side. This is because the moisture is evaporating and taking the latent heat it needs to do so out of your finger. When a gas condenses to a liquid or a liquid solidifies, the latent heat is given out to the environment.

When cloud droplets freeze, latent heat is given off. Because of this heat, the air in the cloud is warmer and less dense than the surrounding air, and so it keeps rising. Once the storm reaches the mature stage and the droplets in the cloud are large enough, they fall as hail or rain. The raindrops or hailstones drag air downward by friction, producing a downdraft. That is, raindrops and hailstones move in the swirling air inside the thunderstorm, and when they start to fall due to the influence of gravity, they drag air with them by friction: The raindrops are falling due to gravity, but the air is descending due to friction with the raindrops. At the same time, the hailstones are getting warmer and melting, and some of the raindrops are evaporating. These processes require latent heat that is taken from the air in the lower part of the cloud. This cools the air, making it more dense, and it sinks. The downdraft is increased by the cold dense air and rushes toward the ground. This is the microburst.

When this cold air hits the ground, it can't form puddles or run down rivers as the rain does—it's got to go somewhere. Cold air bursts from the base of the cloud and hits the ground, and then spreads out horizontally. Some of the air will be pushed upward ahead of the burst. The burst itself only lasts a few minutes, but is very dangerous for a plane trying to land. Imagine coming down the glide slope—the line of approach an airplane takes to land on the runway—with the runway in sight and the plane only a few hundred feet above the ground. Suddenly the plane hits a very strong headwind. Seconds later the aircraft moves out of the headwind into a very strong tailwind. In correcting the aircraft's approach to compensate for the headwind, the pilot puts the plane at completely the wrong angle for the tailwind. The plane will crash or land short of the runway. Some flights have been saved by exceptional pilot skill, but there have been many unfortunate accidents. Landing is the critical time with microbursts: A plane taking off is using full power, so there is less danger. Also, aircraft on the ground don't take off straight into something like a microburst. The pilot waits until it is out of the way.

There are wet microbursts, where the outflow from the cloud can be seen from the rain caught in it, and dry microbursts, where all the rain has evaporated before it reaches the ground. The dry burst can be seen from the dust that is whipped up. In any case, any pilot suspecting that a microburst exists or could develop only has to wait five minutes, and the cloud and any microbursts will be away from the airfield.

We came to understand microbursts in the 1980s, and once we knew the visible signs of microbursts, we could teach the pilots what to look out for and what to expect. Since the 1980s, there haven't been any microburst accidents because the pilots know about them.

Temperature Inversions

Not all wind shears are violent, but they can occur in the oddest places, even when you think the air is too still for any turbulence at all. If an aircraft is taking off early on a clear, windless morning, shortly after take off there will be a small bump as the airplane flies through a temperature inversion. A temperature inversion is an increase in temperature with height. Normally temperature decreases with height. On calm, clear nights, the surface of the earth cools rapidly by radiating heat out into space. Then the cold ground cools the air immediately above it, which in turn cools the air above that. This is a gradual process that keeps going until the sun starts to warm the earth again the next morning. The air in the lower levels is cooled to a temperature below that of the air above it. For instance, suppose at 6 P.M. the surface tem-

*Hail can be tough on planes, but even with
severe hail damage, planes can land safely.*

perature is 20°C (68°F) and the temperature at 1,000 feet is 17°C (63°F)
Overnight the surface cools down to 11°C (52°F), and the air immediately above it is at 11°C (52°F). This cools the air above that and so on.
The temperature at 1,000 feet, however, is still 17°C (63°F), so, instead
of the normal decrease in temperature from the surface upwards, you
have an increase in the lower levels—from 11°C to 17°C (52°F to
63°F)—and above that the temperature falls off with height as normal.
That's the temperature inversion.

Inversions are common on clear, windless mornings and may
extend to 1,000 feet. Winds on the ground below the inversion are usually calm, while above the inversion the wind might be blowing at 40
m.p.h. or 65 k.p.h. As the plane flies into this stronger wind, it is
pushed, and passengers can feel it as a small bump. While the aircraft
has experienced some wind shear–induced turbulence, this is very slight
compared to what we have looked at earlier.

Withstanding Hail

Thunderstorms also can produce hail, which can do a lot of damage to
an aircraft. I once saw a photograph of a Cessna Citation, a small jet aircraft, that flew through hail on the way into Bankstown Airport near
Sydney. The storm was over to the right of the plane, but the hail was
thrown out of the top of the storm and came down in clear air. The pilot
went through it and said it sounded like machine-gun fire. When he put
the aircraft down at Bankstown and got out and looked at it, the entire
leading edge of the wing was flat! The leading edge of the wing is

normally curved, but this was flat. Also flat were the leading edges of the tail plane—the flat, horizontal section at the back of the aircraft that looks like a little wing—and the rudder, which is the vertical section rising from the tail plane. To top it off, the entire nose cone, including the weather radar, had been ripped away.

I showed this photo to a group of fearful fliers. I put a picture of what looked like a demolished aircraft up and said, "Okay, here's a picture of a Cessna Citation that flew through hail—what's the most remarkable thing about it?"

They were in awe, but suddenly somebody said, "It's on its wheels!"

I said, "Yes, it landed quite safely at Bankstown with that amount of damage. The pilot didn't even notice any changes in the flying characteristics of the airplane. He made a normal circuit and landed the aircraft. He didn't declare an emergency—in fact, he had no idea of the extent of damage that had been done to this airplane until he landed and got out and looked at it."

This shows just how robust modern aircraft are—they really are very strong machines.

Lightning

Lightning occurs only in thunderstorms. After all, thunder is only the shockwave produced when lightning heats the air it passes through extremely rapidly. Remarkably, lightning causes very little damage, if any, to airplanes. If lightning hits a plane, the pilot will invariably land to make sure no damage has been done to the aircraft. Usually, though, it doesn't cause any major problems. The aircraft is designed to discharge static electricity very quickly, and it's certainly quite okay for the people inside the aircraft.

A plane works like a Faraday cage, which is named after Michael Faraday, the scientist who discovered that, if you put electricity through a metal box or a metal cage, no matter how strong or high the voltage, anything inside the cage or the box is totally protected from the electricity. That's why cars are safe places to be in thunderstorms—they're metal boxes, and the passengers are in the middle of them. Airplanes are also metal boxes with passengers in the middle of them, so you're still quite safe. Lightning can be very scary for passengers, but it is not a major problem for the aircraft.

Dealing with Snow and Ice

Snow and ice on the airframe change the flying characteristics of the airplane, and so they have to be avoided. Snow can settle on the plane on the ground, and the plane can pick up ice as it flies through cloud. We will look at icing first.

Small ice crystals are not a problem for airplanes, but very cold water is. Water does not have to freeze at 0°C, or 32°F. Pure water that is kept relatively still can remain liquid below 0°C. It needs agitation or small particles such as ice crystals, called "freezing nuclei," before it solidifies. The temperature below which liquid water cannot exist is –40° Celsius and Fahrenheit. (–40° is the magic number at which the Celsius and Fahrenheit scales cross, so it is the same temperature in both scales.) Liquid water below 0°C and above –40°C is called "supercooled water." Supercooled water droplets are common in large convective clouds like cumulonimbus—our friend the thunderstorm—and can also occur in any other cloud that is producing precipitation. If a propeller-driven aircraft flies through one of these clouds, it will disturb these droplets, and they can freeze onto the airframe. In a very short time, the aircraft can pick up a lot of ice that will add weight to the plane and change the shape of the wings. This can be very dangerous. Airframe icing occurs in Australia, but it is more common in the United States due to the geography and the climate there. There are higher mountains, for example, and the land mass of North America goes well into the arctic regions.

Jet aircraft are not affected by ice in this way because the speed at which they fly causes so much frictional heating of the skin of the airplane that any ice simply melts. In fact, the skin of the Concorde gets so hot during flight that the plane stretches a foot or more due to thermal expansion. Smaller, slower, propeller-driven airplanes are affected by ice in clouds, because they are flying at lower levels where ice is more likely to occur and at speeds slow enough for ice to form on the airframe. Because of this greater risk, these aircraft have deicing equipment installed. The leading edge of the wings and the base of the propellers look as if they are covered in black rubber. They are. Along the edge of the wing, inside the rubber, is a series of expanders called "boots." If ice forms on the wing, the deicers are turned on. The deicers make the leading edge expand and contract, breaking the ice away from the wing. Heaters in propeller hubs and other parts of the plane prevent ice from forming in other critical areas.

Usually if an aircraft is picking up ice, the pilot will try to get out of the area. He or she can descend below the freezing level to avoid the ice or supercooled water; climb up to colder air because the colder the air, the more likely it is that the supercooled water drops will have frozen; or try to get out of the cloud. No cloud, no supercooled water.

Snow causes few problems when the plane is in the air, but it can cause problems on the ground. Airplanes require more runway distance when there is snow and ice on runways, as planes taking off are slowed down and planes landing can take longer to slow down. In countries and regions where snowfalls are common, very efficient snow-clearing equipment is used. When the plane is standing at the terminal, snow can build up on the wings, which must be removed before flight. Airport workers will sometimes walk along the wings removing the snow with brooms and deicing sprays. Once the plane is taxiing, the snow has no chance to settle. When pilots are given a taxi clearance, they must move onto the runway and take off with little delay. If they do have to wait and collect another layer of snow, they must go back and have it removed again. Air traffic controllers are aware of this problem and make sure that delays are limited.

Flying in Fog

Meteorologists provide pilots with as much information as possible, so they know what to expect between A and B. If the forecast changes during the flight, the new forecast is passed on by radio to the pilot, who reassesses the flight plan in the light of the new information.

For example, if we have planes coming into Sydney from Los Angeles in the morning, they're going to need to be in Sydney right at six o'clock after the curfew—they can't arrive before then because of noise issues—and that's the most likely time for fog. If Sydney is foggy, the plane can't land and has to go somewhere else. The pilot needs to know if fog is likely to develop at least four hours before the expected arrival time in Sydney, because the flight can then divert to Brisbane, Australia, without using any extra fuel. The plane could still go to Brisbane at a later point when it is closer to Sydney, but it will cost much more in fuel to do so.

These diversions don't happen very often here because we don't get a lot of fog in Sydney. When the fog is not severe, the pilots can land themselves using the instrumentation systems aboard the aircraft. In other parts of the world, such as London, where fogs are more common, automatic landing systems are used. Airports in cities such as London, Paris, New York, Seattle, and Los Angeles have landing systems so sophisticated that pilots can land with no visibility. They are expensive to install, and we don't need them in Australia, but the onboard computers land the plane without the pilot's having to touch the controls at all. The computer can land the plane because it knows where it is and where it's going, even when the human eye can see nothing. The instruments in the aircraft can position the aircraft exactly in relation to the instruments at the airport and put the plane right down onto the ground, take it down the runway, turn off onto the taxiway, and even park it outside the gate without the pilot ever touching the controls. Usually, however, once the plane is on the ground, the pilot takes control again.

The instrumentation on aircraft and at airports today is so efficient that flights can and do arrive and depart in weather that would have closed the airport a few years ago.

Drops in Altitude

Most drops in altitude caused by turbulence and other weather conditions are very slight. A woman in a Fearless Flyers class had gone through a drop of 1,000 feet (304 meters). That's rare. Remember, however, that even though the plane is going down quickly, it is not falling.

A classic example of this is the British Airways Boeing 747 that flew into a cloud of volcanic ash in Indonesia in the mid-1980s. Ash from the volcanic cloud starved the engines of oxygen, all four engines lost power, and the plane descended about 20,000 feet. The pilot let the engines continue turning over and as soon as they were clear of the ash cloud, the engines fired and full control was restored.

One of the passengers on that plane enrolled in the Fearless Flyers course because he had a lot of problems with flying after that incident. It's understandable—that sort of experience would cause problems for anybody—but the thing to remember is that the airplane is still flying, not falling. A plane going down 1,000 feet (305 meters) in turbulence is being pushed by the downdraft, not falling out of the sky. Remember, there's no such thing as an air pocket. The plane that lost all four engines and descended 20,000 feet (6,098 meters), from 35,000 to 15,000 feet (10,671 to 4,573 meters), before the engines worked again was not falling, it was flying. The pilot was gliding the aircraft. As long as the air moves over the wing at the right angle and speed, the wing produces lift and keeps the airplane up. Normally, the engines provide the power to keep the air flowing over the wings, but without engines, the pilot uses gravity to keep the plane in a glide as it descends. In recreational gliders, the pilot uses updrafts to provide the lift.

If you're flying at 35,000 feet and you hit a volcanic ash cloud—which is unlikely now because of new detection systems—and you descend 20,000 feet before the pilot can restart the engines, you're still 15,000 feet above the ground. If you hit the ash at 15,000 feet, and it takes you 20,000 feet to recover, then you've got a problem. Don't forget, however, that the plane is not out of control. The pilot can land the aircraft without power. The space shuttle does it all the time. It descends from outside the atmosphere to land without any engine power at all. It glides. A Boeing 747 is a better glider than the space shuttle.

Volcanoes around the world are monitored since the British Airways incident, and ash cloud warnings are issued if an eruption takes place. The clouds can be seen by weather satellites, so dangerous areas can be identified and pilots can avoid them. There have been many volcanic eruptions since the British Airways incident, but no aircraft have flown into the ash clouds without knowing they were there.

From Problems to Solutions

With all these weather conditions, once you're aware of the problem, it becomes something else: a situation you can do something about. Before we understood what microbursts were, there were microburst accidents. Now we know what microbursts are, how to identify them, and what to look for. Pilots can now avoid them. Likewise, when pilots were first flying over mountains and started experiencing severe turbulence, they called this problem "air pockets" as though the air suddenly disappeared below the aircraft, but now that we understand turbulence, we know that pilots can avoid it or fly successfully through it. Clear air turbulence is the same: When the first planes went way up in the atmosphere and experienced clear air turbulence, the planes were in all sorts of trouble. Now that they know the type of stresses that are going to occur, airplane manufacturers build aircraft to withstand all these.

Every single flight incident, no matter how small, is reported and investigated to see whether anything can be learned from the incident; whether we should change routines or change something else to make it safer to fly. What we end up with is far and away the safest method of transport in the world.

JET MAINTENANCE:
THE FINEST OF
FINE-TOOTH COMBS

The first thing I do when I take my seat—always a window seat!—is to look for the maintenance people, the ground crew. I really scrutinize them. Are they reliable? Bored? Hung over? Intelligent? It seems logical to me that people who do the same thing over and over again, day after day, are bound to get jaded, sloppy, or just plain bored. I worry about the little things that would be easy to miss or let slide during a checkup. And I don't think I'm paranoid—some airplanes really are old. When's the last time somebody checked to make sure the engines were on tight? Or that there's no weakness in the walls of the cabin? With all the financial pressures on airlines, plus the frenzy to be on time, is the maintenance crew as picky as I want them to be?

—Judy Lotas
fearful flier, New York City

Maintaining complex machines like jet aircraft is not a matter of tightening a few screws, oiling a few parts, and off to the proverbial wild blue yonder. It's an entire industry, a business in which relentless scrutiny and meticulous record keeping are the norm, and in which planes and each of their many parts are checked and maintained with tender loving care.

When I was in the throes of my fear of flying, I constantly imagined the plane falling apart in the air because some mechanic hadn't done his or her job. Before I attended the Fearless Flyers course, I had no idea that there was a detailed log kept not only for every jet but for every jet part, and that even nuts and bolts are traceable to FAA-approved manufacturers and suppliers. I hadn't heard that the interiors of jet engines are examined with boroscopes—the industrial equivalent of the instruments used in medicine to examine internal organs—or how jets are completely taken apart and overhauled before being reassembled on a periodic basis.

Most people probably do not know the considerable extent of the free exchange of technical information that goes on behind the scenes between airlines. "In the technical areas, there are no barriers," explains Ken Dunkley, Qantas's manager of mechanical systems engineering at the airport in Sydney, who spends long working days making sure that Qantas's jets are as reliable as possible. "If we see a problem on a Qantas aircraft, we share that with other airlines through either direct contact or the manufacturer. People doing my job at other airlines frequently fax me with tips and other information. In some cases, I have met these people, and in others, I have never met them. We are all colleagues and want to help one another."

Dunkley (who explains aerodynamics in an earlier chapter of this book) says he's pretty typical of the personnel in his sector of Qantas. "Most, if not all, of the people in the engineering support area have been apprentices at Qantas, another airline, or in the case of some of the electronic engineers, a large telecommunications company. They are ex-apprentices who have completed some sort of trade course—an aircraft mechanics course, perhaps—and then gone to university to obtain an engineering degree. Most have spent nearly their whole lives in the aviation industry or some similar engineering organization."

Their common goal is reliability, and Dunkley explains here how they achieve it.

THE ENGINEER'S PERSPECTIVE, WITH KEN DUNKLEY

For the people in the engineering support area, which is divided into several small groups, the first task every morning is to review what happened to all of our aircraft in the last twenty-four hours. Passengers like to see aircraft depart and arrive on time, so the first thing we do in the morning is review the timeliness of departures and arrivals over the last twenty-four hours. Engineering is interested in the technical problems, while other parts of the company review their own special areas—people responsible for checking in passengers, for example, carry out a review of the problems they may have had. The engineering meeting reviews any difficulties that may have occurred in engineering and maintenance, then develops a plan to overcome each problem. The members are responsible for implementing the action and reporting back that they have done so. Things that affect the on-time operation or cause difficulty in safety and efficiency matters pertaining to the fleet are fed into a computer, and a group of engineers monitors the trends. Each month a meeting of specialists from all engineering areas takes place to review these trends.

Because Qantas uses mostly Boeing airplanes, we receive a constant flow of information from Boeing and from the people who make the parts on Boeing airplanes; these are called "service bulletins." We review the service bulletins to see whether we've got that particular problem, whether we can learn from it and prevent a problem from developing, and if there is a better or more economical way of doing it. When we decide to try to implement the suggestions in a service bulletin, we have to find out whether we need more spare parts, whether we have any parts at other stations around the world, and whether those spare parts need repair. We consider these factors as we make the decision about whether or not to implement the bulletin. If we are, how fast are we going to implement it? How crucial is the change? Some bulletins are deemed especially important by Boeing, the American Federal Aviation Administration, or Australia's Civil Aviation Authority. We incorporate those suggestions immediately.

Apart from the bulletins and our own information gathering, there's a constant flow of information from the maintenance workshops. The mechanics sometimes have certain difficulties and come up with things they would like to improve. We've worked closely with them to try to make the place run more efficiently. There is a fair degree of interchange between us and the workshops. Sometimes the mechanics from the workshops spend time working in the engineering support office with the aeronautical engineers to break down the barriers between the departments and make sure we are working as a team. At other times, aeronautical engineers work alongside the mechanics to make sure the engineers fully understand the mechanics' problems.

Routine Problems

Although most of the problems we deal with every day are routine, they can cause aircraft to be delayed. Recently, for example, one of the 767s was delayed in Jakarta because of an oil leak. The problem in the airplane was relatively minor, but it was fairly difficult to fix because the problem was in the tail. That meant they had to go get a cherry picker to reach up to the tail of the airplane, remove a fairly difficult panel to get access to this component, and tighten up a little fitting. All this resulted in a late departure; several flights were canceled, so there probably were some upset passengers.

*During the D check, an aircraft is completely
taken apart, inspected, and put back together.*

The problem was minor, but from the company's point of view, it was a major problem, because a whole bunch of passengers were not happy. The next question we ask ourselves is, what do we do to make sure that doesn't happen again? So I wouldn't call this problem mundane—I'd call it a relatively insignificant problem from a technical point of view, and a relatively significant problem from the company's point of view.

A Constant Series of Checks

There's a whole series of checks on aircraft, ranging from the "A" check to the "D" check. There is no "B" check; we stopped that years ago because we were able to refine our procedures and incorporate some of the B check work into the A check and some into the C check.

The A check is done every 600 flying hours, and the D check is done every 25,000 flying hours. Each check gets more and more complex. The preflight check is done before each flight and is fairly simple, like walking around your car to make sure all the wheels are there and nothing has fallen off. The pilot and the ground engineer walk around the airplane to make sure the wheels look okay, the brakes look okay, and there's nothing else that's obviously wrong with the airplane.

The A check is quite complicated. It takes fifteen to twenty people about a day to do, and a whole range of things are checked. We grease various parts of the airplane, inspect certain things, closely look at the brakes and the wheels, and inspect the parts of the cabin of the airplane that get the most wear and tear, like the galleys and toilets. There's also a heavier maintenance check called the "Super A," which is done every 2,500 hours of flying time and employs forty-five to fifty people for two or three days.

Every 4,000 or 6,000 hours, depending on the aircraft type, the aircraft is grounded for about six days for a C check, and this requires ninety to a hundred people. Again, that gets to be fairly complicated. Every 25,000 hours, ninety to a hundred workers perform the D check for about twenty-five days. In this check, all the landing gear is taken out; people get inside the fuel tanks and inspect the insides; and areas that suffer a lot of corrosion, like toilets and galleys, are taken out and inspected. In a D check, the most intensive, we strip the aircraft down to a bare shell. We inspect that bare shell and all the parts, then put it all back together again. It is quite a task! When you look at the aircraft halfway through a D check, you wonder how it will ever go back together again. But it does — in about five days with only two shifts per day, the aircraft is reassembled, tested, and pronounced ready for service.

When you buy the airplane, you get a manual with it as you do with a car. It states the minimum amount of maintenance you have to do, according to legal requirements. But we do far more work than that, and so do all airlines, because we want the aircraft to appeal to passengers. We want the planes to be nice, clean, and good-looking — and reliable. The work that we, and every other airline, do is far in excess of the legal requirement.

Handling Parts with Kid Gloves

Aircraft parts are horrendously expensive. This is mostly because of the manufacturer's original development costs; before a part is ever sold to an airline, the manufacturer must perform a huge number of tests to prove to the FAA or CAA that the part performs as it should. Further, that huge development cost is absorbed from a relatively small number of airplanes. The Boeing 747 has been far more successful than Boeing ever envisaged, so the company has made more than a thousand 747s now. That is far fewer than the number of cars General Motors makes in a single day, so that cost is amortized over a fairly small number of production parts, which makes the cost per part quite high.

For this reason, people are very careful with the parts. In the same way that people paint their houses to protect them, the parts are painted with several coats of special paint. They are handled very carefully, housed in special areas that only approved people can access, and stored in well-padded boxes.

The best part to give as an example is the wheel, because most of us have cars. An aircraft wheel is more complicated than a car wheel, as the hub on which the tire is mounted is divided in two halves bolted together. That is made from aluminum, and there are some steel parts where the wheel connects to the brake. We can tell when the tire is worn out in the same way you do on your car: when there is no tread left. When the tire is worn out, it is taken off and sent away to the tire manufacturer for a stringent inspection, and if it passes, it may be retreaded for a limited number of times. Meanwhile, the aluminum hub is inspected for cracks and corrosion by a series of specialist mechanics. If there is the most minor blemish, the hub is scrapped. If it passes inspection, it is reassembled with another tire and refitted to an aircraft. Every tenth tire change, we go even further and remove all the steel parts for a separate "strip" check in which we strip all the paint from the aluminum hub and carry out even more detailed checks. The hub is then repainted with a special hard epoxy paint, reassembled with a tire, left to stand for twelve hours to ensure that it does not lose any pressure, and returned to service.

For another example, the landing gear is taken out every 25,000 hours. This is a large, complicated, expensive piece of equipment. It's separated into its component parts, the paint is taken off, and all the steel parts are inspected for cracks and corrosion. If there's any corrosion on the bushes—a bush is a cylindrical piece of brass at a pivot point—new bushes are installed. Finally, the whole thing is repainted and reassembled, which takes lots and lots of work hours and material costs.

Because the 747 is so big, it has four landing-gear legs with four wheels each under the center of the body and one landing-gear leg with two wheels at the nose. Each landing gear leg is assembled from many parts, each of which is very precisely manufactured from the highest quality steel. All these parts are assembled to make a landing gear that can be retracted into the body when the aircraft takes off and extended again when the aircraft is ready to land. Every five years we remove the entire five landing-gear legs from each aircraft and install a newly overhauled set. The removed items are then completely dismantled and inspected, and if they are still satisfactory, reassembled for installation on another aircraft. All of this costs about AUS $1 million (US $650,000), not even including the wheels and brakes!

Maintaining the Engines

Engines are constantly monitored. Quite big and expensive, the typical engine costs about AUS $5 million (US $3.2 million) and weighs about five tons. One of my colleagues monitors engine performance all day

An airplane's engines, such as that of the
Boeing 737 pictured here, are meticulously maintained.

long. This engineer plots how much fuel an engine is using, what temperatures are being recorded inside, and so on. Some aircraft automatically transmit this data to us as they're flying, and a computer records it. Other aircraft have the information telexed back to main base after each flight to be entered into the database. If a trend is developing, the computer points that out to us. In addition, we regularly look inside the engine with a boroscope to inspect all the integral parts. If we see a problem, we can change the aircraft's flight schedule to extend the time at the maintenance base and remove the engine to allow the problem to be rectified. The last thing we want is to have an engine problem at some place other than our main base, where we have all our spares.

Meticulous Record Keeping

Cyclic components, the ones we keep forever and constantly overhaul, are closely watched. For important cyclic components like engine fan blades and hydraulic pumps, we keep an entire history from the first day of service. Other items such as nuts and bolts have a traceable history back to the original FAA-approved supplier. We keep a record of the life of every component assembly that we've owned and everything that's ever been done to it: who overhauled it, why they did it, where they did it, what parts they replaced, where the new parts came from, and who put it back on the airplane.

Similarly, each aircraft's complete history is carefully recorded on what is called a technical log. Everything that happens to the aircraft is put in the log. When an aircraft lands at Bangkok and has a certain defect, the defect and the rectification are entered in the computer database. The database contains the log history of each of our airplanes since

105

the beginning of time. Each aircraft has a registration the same as a car has, so first you have to know which airplane you're talking about. The database is arranged so that you go into the aircraft fleet type, say, 747-400, ask for the log of the plane you're interested in, and arrange the data in whatever way you need. For example, you can have it arranged chronologically or by station or what airport the plane has been to. Another log covers the cabin of the aircraft—whether the coffeemaker is working, the oven's hot enough, all that sort of stuff—problems that affect passenger comfort rather than technical performance.

Scrutinizing Older Planes

Our computer programs constantly monitor planes as they get older. Meanwhile, the engineers review the work cards. Everything that's done on the airplane is done on a job card, which notes both the function performed and any defects found, and that card has to be signed by the mechanic doing the job. All this information is entered into a computer. Any time you want, you can use a coding system, press a button, and ask for all information on landing gear. That way you can see if a trend has developed over the past year. If, for example, we've had more tire problems in the last couple of months than we'd had earlier, we ask why that is happening and look for a solution.

Of course, different operating patterns in the aircraft can affect it, too. An aircraft that operates internationally does an average of two and a half flights per day, so there are two and a half passengers getting in each seat per day, and the cargo doors only get opened two and a half times per day. A plane that operates domestically, on the other hand, might have five flights a day, so there are five people in and out of seats per day, the cargo door is opened five times per day, and the plane is going to wear out more quickly. You've got to grease planes that fly on twice as many flights twice as often. We're constantly reviewing things like that.

In addition to all of our checks, there are also Boeing representatives here who watch over their planes because we've principally got Boeing airplanes. If we had Airbuses, we'd have Airbus representatives. These representatives are looking after their company's interests, and they give their company the information that they see developing as time rolls on. The manufacturers collect all this information, just as we do, and they put it together and publish it in a service bulletin that allows us to learn from the experience of other airlines, who may have even older airplanes than we do.

Bogus Parts

Avoiding bogus airplane parts is a real challenge for the whole industry. We and every other airline are very aware of them, and we've gotten more and more strict. Each part that comes from outside Qantas has to be certified as a genuine part made by the preapproved authorized manufacturer, and all the paperwork must be correct.

We are scrupulous about this. Just recently, we desperately wanted some parts, and the parts arrived. But the paperwork wasn't correct, and the serial number was missing. It was quite obvious that this part was not a bogus part, but it was crucial that the paperwork be correct. The parts had to be sent all the way back to the manufacturer in the United States so that they could say, "Yes, I really made this part, and this is the serial number," and then check a box on a piece of paper and send the whole lot back to us again. We were desperate to have it, but we had to have the paperwork correct.

Bogus work parts usually come from two sources. One is airplanes that have been scrapped or damaged; people sometimes get hold of the parts on these planes and try to sell them without declaring their true source or their history. The other source is people who take some real parts, measure them up, which is fairly easy to do, figure out what they are made of, and make new pieces according to their version of the original drawing. We're very strict about making sure that we don't buy any of these parts.

Bogus parts don't necessarily come from Third World countries. We've had parts that weren't approved that came from the United States. In this particular case, the manufacturer of a large assembly had specified a small component in the assembly and given it a part number. The drawing for this small component specified that it be supplied from certain sources that the large manufacturer had specifically approved, but an unapproved manufacturer started to supply this small component and to give it the original drawing number, even though this manufacturer was not approved to do so. As soon as we became aware of this problem, we scrapped the entire stock.

There are two associations worldwide that help airlines be vigilant about bogus parts. All of the airlines outside the United States belong to an association called the International Air Transport Association, known as IATA, and its U.S. equivalent is the Air Transport Association, or ATA. IATA and ATA work with all the airlines, making sure that information that affects matters of safety is shared among them.

Backups for Failed Systems

Every airplane has a built-in degree of redundancy in its mechanical systems, and there is always more than one way of doing something. Boeing, Airbus, and other airplane manufacturers ask themselves, "What if this happened . . . ? What's the backup?" There is a backup. For example, on the 747, which has five sets of landing gear, there are two ways of lowering the landing gear: hydraulically and by using gravity. In addition, the landing gear is divided into different hydraulic systems, so if one hydraulic system fails, then only some of the landing gear needs to use the backup system.

In fact, there are backups to backups to backups. There are three ways of braking, so if by chance the hydraulic system that works the brakes fails, there's another system. And if that fails, there's another system. In contrast, there are very few backups in your car. Modern cars have two hydraulic systems, but older cars didn't. Aircraft have multiple hydraulic systems that give them many different ways of applying the brakes. Likewise, each wheel is controlled by two separate anti-skid systems, and in the flight controls, there are several sets of controls to handle the pitching or rolling motion of the airplane. Redundancy upon redundancy upon redundancy is built into the airplane. Not only that, there's also a very cautious driver up front called the pilot who won't let the airplane take off or will divert to another airport if he or she becomes unhappy about anything. Furthermore, pilots have a very strict set of rules produced by Boeing and Qantas and implemented by the CAA and FAA, which says that pilots cannot depart if everything is not working perfectly.

TAKING THE BULL
BY THE HORNS:
WAYNE NORMAN'S STORY

Almost all aspects of flying scare me, starting with being off the ground. When my feet are on the floor of the plane cabin, I absolutely feel *that they aren't on the ground!*

—Judy Fayard
fearful flier, Paris, France

When Wayne Norman stood up and gave a brief, uplifting speech to 250 people at the Fearless Flyers reunion dinner in late 1996 at a hotel near the Sydney airport, I'd never have guessed that, before he had taken the course, he had found it impossible to address a gathering even of the twenty people who worked for him. And from the way he spoke about the triumph of taking flying lessons in a single-engine Piper Warrior, I certainly wouldn't have taken him for someone who had been so paralyzed by fear at the thought of getting on an airplane that for years he had preferred to spend up to fourteen hours behind the wheel of a car driving to the holiday destinations that his wife, Lynn, and four children had flown to.

Wayne Norman's recovery was touch and go. Not having flown in close to thirty years, he was nearly unable to board the Fearless Flyers graduation flight in November 1995. He went to the airport intending to bid farewell to his fellow classmates but "somehow" managed to walk on board with them. He didn't regret it. "Back in Sydney, after the graduation flight, I was on top of the moon," remembers Wayne Norman, now forty-five. "I had accomplished something that I thought I would never again do till the day I died."

His story could easily have had a depressing ending. Norman, who in spite of his fears has been fascinated by airplanes all his life, was seventeen and working on a student pilot's license at the airport at Bankstown, the town where he grew up, just south of Sydney, when his fears began. He now believes that his fears were connected to the nervous breakdown his father, who used to go flying with him, suffered around that time. Suddenly the heights Norman was used to seemed dizzying, and he started having panic attacks. Soon, merely the fear of having a panic attack was enough to stop him in his tracks, a familiar phenomenon to anyone who has ever suffered from a panic disorder.

His fears soon were not limited to airplanes. The sight of the Sydney's lofty Harbour Bridge or Centrepoint Tower was enough to upend him emotionally. "Three or four floors of a building was the most I could handle," he recounts. "Even at two floors, I'd get stressed. That fear escalated over the next thirty years, and I got to the point that, even though I'd always loved airplanes, I'd watch the planes take off at the airport, and I'd relate that to the height off the ground. It would spark all these feelings of anxiety, terror, and frustration." Those feelings in turn brought on unpleasant sensations that Norman describes as "a tightening of the stomach, shaking, perspiring, and feeling out of control."

Norman eventually stopped flying altogether and began taking the car on vacations while the rest of his family flew. "My wife used to beg me to fly her somewhere, say, for our anniversary, and I'd always find an excuse not to," he says. "It's amazing how many excuses you can find—time, work, no means of transport when you get there. . . ." Had his fear affected only his travel habits, Norman might not have felt compelled to seek help, but his anxiety about not being able to fly was "knocking him around" in other ways. His self-esteem and confidence took a nosedive. He was plagued by awful imaginings, such as being at great heights with no signs of support, and could not block out the intrusive thoughts and images in his head. Problems that would normally be manageable in his job as director of a kitchen manufacturing company in Sydney were blown out of proportion for him, and addressing his employees as a group became impossible.

Norman was taking a course designed to help people change their ways of thinking to overcome phobias when his mother told him about hearing Fearless Flyers coordinator Glenda Philpott on the radio. Norman signed on, but he admits he was a tough nut to crack. What made the most difference, however, was the support of the women running the course. "At one point I threw in the towel," sighs Norman. "I wrote a three- or four-page letter to Glenda saying that the anxiety about getting on an airplane was overwhelming and that I couldn't go through with the course. I couldn't sleep and couldn't function at work because I was thinking about it so much." The savvy Philpott and her colleagues neither accepted his resignation nor pressured him to complete the course. "They acted as if it was no big deal," Norman relates, as if still amazed. "They said, 'Okay, don't do it, but because of your friends in the course, try to complete the last couple of sessions and go to the airport to say goodbye.'"

Norman agreed to start taking it one step at a time. Qantas manager of mechanical systems engineering Ken Dunkley, a volunteer with Fearless Flyers, took both Norman and a member of the class with posttraumatic stress syndrome from experiences in the Vietnam War under his wing. Scheduling desensitization sessions to augment the regular Fearless Flyers classes, Dunkley took the pair from parked plane to parked plane, spending hours sitting inside the planes with them, talking about the technical aspects of flying.

When Norman left his home in Orangeville, a semi-rural area about sixty miles west of Sydney, to drive to Sydney Airport on the day of the graduation flight, he told his wife that he honestly didn't know whether he would return after a couple of hours or a couple of days. He figured he had the choice of waving his friends off and coming home; getting on the plane, having a panic attack during the flight, and taking the train home in a day or two; or completing the mission and returning later in the afternoon.

What helped him, Norman thinks, was that Glenda Philpott introduced him to Qantas captain Lyn Williams, who would be their pilot on the graduation flight. "He was very confident, very strong-looking, and looked like someone you could trust and rely on," Norman says.

Other people also offered support. Brenda Larsson, a volunteer and herself a graduate of the course (along with me) in April 1994, came up to Norman before the final relaxation exercises before the flight and handed him a golf ball. She suggested he could hang onto it and squeeze it if he got nervous. (He still has it and takes it along on flights as a sort of talisman, even though he doesn't squeeze it anymore.) And once Norman found himself walking onto the plane, Karen Tomlinson—a volunteer and former fearful flier whose own story is on page 79—sat next to him in the business class section where the class had been seated and talked him through much of the flight to Melbourne.

As patient as Tomlinson was with him, the flight was a series of emotional fits and starts for Norman. During takeoff, he insisted that Tomlinson pull the shade on the window because of his fear of heights. Then, when pilot Williams invited him to visit the cockpit, Norman shuffled into the front of the plane, eyes downcast, not daring to look up from the lights on the instrument panel in the foreground. Williams gently suggested that Norman take a look down at Albury, the small city that was clearly visible below. "After the initial gasp, it became very interesting," says Norman of an action that just thinking about would have made him reel. "I went back down to my seat, opened the window, and enjoyed the second half of the flight immensely." On the way back, Norman's window shade was up when the plane took off.

As exultant as he was back on terra firma, Norman knew he had to take seriously the advice from his instructors that he fly as frequently as possible. A week later, he and Lynn went away for a weekend on Australia's Gold Coast. The exercise, he says, was not just to prove he could fly but to try to start making up to her all the years he'd been unable to travel with her. He also started asking friends to join him as a passenger on a series of chartered sightseeing flights on an old World War II DC-3 out of Bankstown Airport south of Sydney. Before long, he had thirteen of these flights under his belt. "Each flight started off with this anxiety, but once the plane left the ground, I was fine," he says.

Norman picked up where he'd left off at the age of seventeen, and started taking flying lessons once again at Bankstown Airport. "I'm still very nervous every time I go out," he admits. "But I'm determined to be able to feel confident flying myself." The man who once drove hours on end to catch up with his family on vacations wants to be able to fly the whole family wherever they go together in the future.

Meanwhile, every time he goes up with his flight instructor and conquers his initial anxiety, Norman says, "What used to be a mountain is now a hill. After I land and turn the motor off, I get a feeling of exhilaration, like 'Done it! You beauty!' I feel revved up. Every time I do it—and I feel I must do it as frequently as possible until it becomes like driving a car—my self-esteem rises considerably. I feel twice the size when I get off the plane as when I got on."

FLIGHT ATTENDANTS: WAITRESSES IN THE SKY OR COMMANDOS?

*The flight attendants started showing us
how to put on life jackets, and I was horrified.
I thought, obviously there is a chance this
plane is going to crash!*

—Donald Evans
Fearless Flyers class of October 1979

THE AUTHOR INTERVIEWS MARIE WILLIAMS, RETIRED QANTAS CHIEF FLIGHT ATTENDANT

For some tremulous travelers, flight attendants can seem like The Enemy because they are the people who, standing up to brief passengers on safety and emergency procedures, remind us that planes are not infallible. For others, attendants seem like saviors, because they supply those calming cocktails that fearful fliers often swill in a desperate attempt to blunt their fears.

For too many members of the public, however, flight attendants are the objects of condescension and even derision. How many times, for example, have you heard someone, with a smirk or a wink, lump female attendants into the "Coffee, Tea, or Me?" category of employee? Or heard flight attendants referred to as waitresses or waiters in the sky? Indeed, I heard a tale from one attendant about a man in business class who declared to her, "You're only here to serve me a meal!"

The man might have thought twice about his remark had he known that this woman and her colleagues are trained to deal with hijackers, put out fires, evacuate a plane in ninety seconds with virtually no cabin visibility, and perform many other maneuvers. Indeed, they are put through exercises on emergency procedures and quizzed regularly and relentlessly by the airlines until they could write a book about flight safety in their sleep. The Mr. Rudes of this world might also be humbled to remember that, even if an emergency is unlikely, their very lives could be in the hands of the same flight attendants whose authority they're undermining—or whose bottoms they're thinking of pinching.

That flight attendants are very much more than glorified waitresses and waiters is driven home with panache by Marie Williams. Williams, who started her career with Qantas in 1973 as what was then referred to as a "flight hostess," retired in 1991 as a chief flight attendant and now teaches Fearless Flyers classes. It is Williams' job during the course to explain how thoroughly attendants are trained. And while it can be a bit unnerving for fearful fliers with overactive imaginations to get a tour of the Qantas flight attendant training facilities—complete with swimming pool, evacuation slides, and inflated life rafts—they leave knowing that flight attendant training is serious business, and that their lives are in good hands.

A Variety of Vocations Combined

As Williams explains, attendants must wear many hats. They must be mediators when arguments break out between passengers; they must be safety officers, psychiatrists, nurses, babysitters, interpreters, and janitors. That's apart from looking well groomed at all times, remaining pleasant while serving meals and drinks, and advising passengers about safety. Most important of all, Williams stresses, "You must be able to swim well, be strong enough to open doors and exits, pull life rafts from overhead if applicable, block exits, redirect passengers, and know how to control a crowd."

Williams remembers the days when attendants were known as "flight hostesses" and when her main duties *were* serving meals, cleaning the toilets, and doing paperwork. It was the male "stewards" who were responsible for doing the heavy work like opening exits, and the women were known as "assists." Williams also worked through the era when stewardesses would be weighed regularly, but not the stewards. "Female flight attendants weren't there for safety in those days," she recalls.

That all changed. In 1983, flight hostesses and stewards became "flight attendants," and Qantas began employing an equal number of male and female flight attendants, offering both the same promotional opportunities. Now, attendants who are flying long-haul flights must go through eight weeks of training, including emergency and medical procedures. They have to dive in the swimming pool and show that they can swim strongly, and know every aspect of each aircraft they will be flying aboard and where every piece of emergency equipment is located, from flashlights to fire extinguishers. They must be able to open exits, and direct passengers down the slides and into life rafts or away from the planes. In fact, using volunteer passengers to fill the seats in mock-ups of the jets, the airlines teach attendants how to evacuate a full plane in ninety seconds, using half the available exits. That's with lots of smoke, some fire, and deafening noise to make the situation all the more realistic. When this exercise is completed, each attendant has an area she or he checks again before abandoning the plane, just to make sure everyone is out.

Recurrent Training

This is not a one-shot deal, either. For two days every year, attendants are given recurrent training in emergency procedures, such as what to do if there is a fire outside the exit or a jammed door, and a written exam. "You can only get two questions wrong out of a hundred," Williams says. "And you can't fly until you pass that test." On top of this, the airlines give spot quizzes. Every several weeks, an attendant reporting for work will be taken aside and asked to answer about a dozen questions, which differ every time. Again, if they don't pass that test, they don't fly, and their pay is docked until they can pass. "I was unnerved by this at first," Williams admits. "But it makes you aware of emergency procedures, and they stay in your mind. I remember that once when the landing gear wouldn't come down and we had to fly over the tower, my mind went straight to the emergency procedures. When I spoke to the other attendants afterward, they all said the same thing." (The plane landed safely.)

A Sampling of the Spot-Quiz Questions
Flight Attendants Must Answer

These spot quizzes are called "pre-departure checks." A cabin crew member is not checked prior to every trip but probably every few weeks. The questions fall into two categories: operation of onboard equipment and "what-if" emergency procedures. Possible questions about equipment involve handing the crew member a piece of safety equipment and asking him or her to demonstrate its use. This includes fire extinguishers, smoke hoods, portable oxygen bottles (for revival of passengers), and even handcuffs for restraining violent passengers. (These last are standard on all airlines and can be used only with the consent of the pilot.)

The "what-ifs" can be broken down into generic questions covering all aircraft types, and flight attendants are asked what they would do

- If the aircraft experiences a sudden loss of cabin pressure?
- If a fire starts in a galley oven or in a toilet because of a careless smoker?

- If a passenger becomes violent or abusive?
- If a passenger shows symptoms of hypoxia (oxygen deficiency)?

Other questions relate to aircraft by specific type, such as the 767-300 or the 747-400.

Each aircraft varies in the type and location of its emergency equipment, the operation of its emergency exit doors, and other features. While variations are sometimes not great, this information is nonetheless essential. A flight attendant will fail at the pre-departure check if he or she is uncertain of the answers to these questions. Here are some possible questions:

1) You are operating on a 767-300. A passenger alerts you to a toilet fire. What call do you make on the cabin interphone to alert both the flight and cabin crew?
   The handpiece of the aircraft interphone differs between the 747 and 767. Crew must know, without hesitation, the correct button to press to alert other crew members to an emergency situation.

2) You are sitting on the jumpseat at the overwing exit on a 747-400. You are doing a silent review of emergency procedures. For example, if the aircraft were to land with the landing gear having failed, what would you do?
   The attendant would check outside the window for fire. If there is no fire, he or she would disarm the nearest door and open it so that the slide at the overwing does not interfere with slides at other doors, which is likely if landing gear has collapsed.

3) Where is the 3.3-pound (1.5-kilogram) fire extinguisher located in the forward galley on the 747-400 aircraft?
   The forward-facing wall, right-hand side.

4) What are the indicators that a door is properly armed on a 767 aircraft?
   Three yellow placards.

5) If the airplane ditches (makes a water landing), who initiates the evacuation once the aircraft has come to a complete standstill?
   Cabin crew.

6) You are taxiing into a terminal, and you notice a fire in one of the engines. What do you do?
   Contact the flight deck.

7) The aircraft has commenced its takeoff roll. You notice a fire in one of the engines. What do you do?

You do not contact the flight deck yet, as the takeoff is a critical time. A flight attendant, having noticed a problem or having been alerted by a passenger to one, is taught to use his or her judgment in contacting the flight deck. Crew members are not to contact the flight deck during the "critical phase" of a takeoff or landing. In other words, once the takeoff roll has commenced, the flight crew would not answer a call from the cabin crew until all their procedures were followed and the flight was airborne. Likewise, during the landing, once the flight crew has lowered the landing gear, contact is avoided until the aircraft has landed and slowed.

8) Would you use the upper deck doors on a 747-400 to evacuate passengers in the case of a ditching or a land evacuation? *No for the ditching in the water, yes for land evacuation.*

9) Where are the infant life jackets located on the 767, 747-200, 747-300, and 747-400?
Location varies with each plane.

10) Where are the radio survival beacons (to transmit distress signals) located on these same aircraft?
Again, it varies.

Handling Fearful Fliers

Although attendants' training even extends to handling violent passengers, one subject that most are *not* versed in is how to deal with fearful fliers. "Before I started working with Fearless Flyers, I was not aware of what some passengers went through," says Marie Williams. "A lot of people hide their fear. They drink too much or they sit there petrified, but the average attendant isn't aware of it. There's no way we could figure out, for example, how somebody like you would react to aircraft noises."

It is Williams' hope that flight attendants of the future will be taught how to help fearful fliers. Meanwhile, she works hard to reassure fearful fliers about how strenuously the crews are trained, and to get them to focus on the safety roles of the attendants more than their service duties. Relates Williams, "I say, 'What is more important to you, the meals or whether we can get you out in an emergency?'"

And, by the way, how *does* an attendant deal with Mr. and Ms. Rudes during a flight? According to Williams, "You have to be charming, be nice, and smile—then go into the nearest toilet, silently scream, count to ten, then come out smiling."

AIR TRAFFIC CONTROL: THE "PROTECTIVE HAND"

When we're stacked up over Chicago, and it's milk out my window and the plane's being buffeted by winds that are leading up to a snowstorm, and the captain says, "Uh . . . ladies and gentlemen, we're going to be delayed a little bit in our landing here at O'Hare . . ." I go crazy. I don't trust the people in charge to keep the planes sorted out. There's no visual way for the pilot to keep us from ramming into another plane, and the stacking thing seems really ominous. Plus, I can't see anything, though I have a compulsion to look out the window. It really is hell.

—Judy Lotas
fearful flier, New York City

After seeing for myself how calm and collected the inside of an air traffic control tower was — a far cry from my imagined den of chain-smokers a hair's breadth away from cracking up at the console — the biggest surprise about this area of aviation was its immense scope and complexity. Far from being the whole of air traffic control operations, the tower we see from the plane at the airport is only the tip of the iceberg. Air traffic control is a worldwide network wherein each plane is a bit like a baton in a relay, handed over from one section of monitored airspace to the next as it flies to its destination. From the moment it leaves its gate to the moment it docks at its destination, everything that airplane does is watched by controllers. Twenty-four hours a day, somebody is monitoring every flight to make sure it's on course and doesn't get too close to another airplane.

Alan Dukes, an air traffic controller at the Sydney Airport, taught me during Fearless Flyers to think of air traffic control as a "protective hand" not only over my plane but over all planes. In this chapter, he provides an in-depth look at the vastness and intricacy of the air traffic control system. And as an annex to this chapter, Ron Morgan, director of air traffic control for the Federal Aviation Administration in the United

States, explains why you need not fear flying into very busy airports, such as those in New York, Los Angeles, or Chicago, which have a high volume of air traffic.

THE AIR TRAFFIC CONTROLLER'S PERSPECTIVE, WITH ALAN DUKES

An air traffic controller has to be one part juggler, one part chess genius Bobby Fischer, one part traffic police officer, and one part bookworm to keep track of all the regulations. Air traffic control is one of the most exciting and exacting careers in the world: It's a "zero defect" occupation, in which the job has to get done right the first time. Air traffic control is a worldwide network that helps the aviation industry maintain its extremely high safety record of air travel. It monitors the position of aircraft and ensures that the minimum specified distance between aircraft is not infringed upon. This minimum distance is called "separation."

Air traffic control is like a relay race in which each aircraft is like the baton. Aircraft are handed off from one controller to the next, from taxiing all the way until the aircraft arrives at its destination and parks at the terminal. We tell the pilot where to go and at what altitude to fly to make sure the plane remains safely separated from other aircraft. At all times, everything the aircraft does is approved by air traffic control. Most airline aircraft are subject to air traffic control. There are some areas, however, where no air traffic control service is provided.

The Tower

Some people think that all air traffic controllers work in the tower at the airport. This couldn't be further from the truth! The control tower is only the most visible symbol of air traffic control. The other 95 percent of air traffic control takes place away from the tower in special air traffic control centers. These centers don't have to be located at an airport; in fact, most new centers look like ordinary office complexes from the outside. The control tower must be located at the airport because the primary method of separation used here is visually separating the aircraft by looking out the window. Each tower has two types of controller: surface movement controllers and aerodrome controllers.

Surface Movement Controllers

Surface movement controllers are also known as "ground controllers," because their job is to control all aircraft and vehicles on the ground, moving around on the taxiways, and entering or leaving the airline terminals. Taxiways are like roads that lead from the terminal to the runway. Surface movement controllers are like traffic police officers. They decide which aircraft must give way or stop at an intersection of taxiways, and they tell aircraft which taxiways to follow so that they can get from the terminal to the runway or from the runway to the terminal.

Aerodrome Controllers

"Aerodrome" is a synonym for airport, and the aerodrome controller is responsible for all aircraft landing and departing on the runways. The aerodrome controller's primary job is to clear aircraft for landing and takeoff while making sure that a very strict set of operating procedures is followed to guarantee separation. Doing this job well requires total concentration and an acute sense of timing and judgment. This is one of the higher-pressure jobs in air traffic control.

The aerodrome controller has to guarantee that the spacing between departing aircraft satisfies the minimum distance required by the radar controller in the terminal control center, who oversees the area around the airport. The aerodrome controller also has to ensure separation between the arriving aircraft and those wishing to depart. Sometimes things don't go according to plan, and an arriving aircraft needs to be told to "go around." This means that the aircraft climbs back up and is given instructions to go back and rejoin the queue, or line, of arriving airplanes. A go-around is not an emergency procedure, but a controlled, safe procedure to ensure separation and safety.

In weather such as fog, low clouds, or storms, we increase the space required between arriving airplanes because the tower may not be able to see the aircraft. Pilots can fly the aircraft in cloud or fog by using special instruments that give them all the information they need to fly the planes. These instruments are so sophisticated that the plane can, at certain airports, land in conditions of almost zero visibility. In fog, in poor visibility, or at night, controllers in the tower use special radar equipment to watch aircraft as they move around the airport.

Another important duty for an aerodrome controller is to separate aircraft from wake turbulence, the vortex created from each wingtip when a plane is flying. The bigger the aircraft, the more intense the vortex, so air traffic controllers must leave more space clear behind a 747 than we would behind a light aircraft so that the wake turbulence from the 747 has time to dissipate. Otherwise, that turbulence can disturb the equilibrium of the plane behind it.

Terminal Area Controllers

The terminal area covers roughly a thirty- to fifty-mile (forty-eight- to eighty-kilometer) radius around the airport. There generally is a high number of aircraft operating within it, and there is a high level of complexity due to the mixture of arriving and departing aircraft.

Along with aerodrome controllers, terminal area controllers have the highest-pressure jobs in air traffic control. The terminal area controller normally works in a control center using radar to see aircraft and make sure they stay separated. Where the tower controller looks after the aircraft at a single airport, the terminal area controller may have several airports within his or her area of responsibility. Furthermore, the terminal area controller does not need to be located at the airport. Advanced communications equipment allows the control center to be located hundreds of miles away from the airport. For example, the terminal area control service for Canberra, the capital of Australia, is performed by controllers who work in a radar center near Melbourne, about 530 miles (850 kilometers) away.

Only a limited amount of room is available in the terminal area to maneuver aircraft to accomplish the required separation. Due to the complexity of the traffic and the precision required, there are different terminal area controllers for arriving and departing aircraft: approach controllers and departures controllers.

The terminal area controllers, like the tower controller, control aircraft during the most critical phases of flight. This means that they need to be aware of both the aircraft's operational requirements and the workload of the pilots, who are under the most pressure during takeoffs and landings to make sure that all systems on the aircraft are operating correctly. Terminal area controllers work very closely with the tower controllers to achieve the maximum number of aircraft arriving and departing from the airport. In Sydney in 1998, government legislation limits the total number of arriving or departing aircraft in any hour to eighty.

The reason we try to achieve the maximum movements per hour at the airport is to reduce delays both for aircraft in the air and for aircraft waiting to depart. If aircraft are delayed arriving, then this delays departing flights, and the delays can then spread out throughout the airlines' networks. Sydney is the busiest airport in Australia, so if there are delays for aircraft into or out of Sydney, then the flights around the rest of Australia are also delayed. But of course, safety is our priority in all operations.

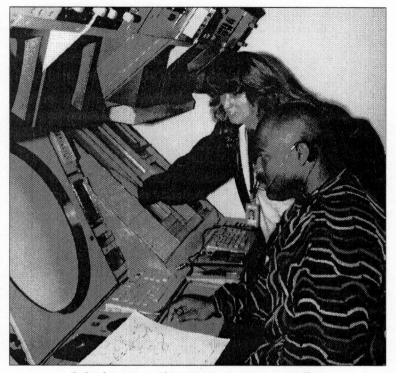

*Federal Aviation Administration en route controllers,
who make sure aircraft stay separated as they fly
to their destinations, concentrate at the console.*

En Route Controllers

En route controllers take the planes over from the terminal area controllers and have the largest areas to monitor, the sectors of airspace a plane goes through once it leaves the terminal area and is on its way to its destination. (*En route* is French for "on the way.") Due to the size of the areas they control, en route controllers have some areas where they can see aircraft on radar and others that are outside radar coverage. In oceanic areas, a controller may be responsible for an area covering many thousands of square miles. Another en route controller may operate an area that is only thirty by forty miles (forty-eight by sixty-four kilometers), which feeds aircraft into a terminal area. The size of the area controlled depends on its location relative to major airports and the number of aircraft that will be operating in the area. The higher the number of aircraft, the smaller the area allocated to each controller. Each piece of airspace is called a "sector," and en route controllers are often referred to as "sector controllers."

A Worldwide Network of Air Traffic Control

In terms of air traffic, Australia controls approximately one tenth of the surface area of the Earth. Our area covers all of the Australian mainland and many hundreds of miles of ocean to the east and west. To the south, our area stretches down to the Antarctic territories. As you fly from one country's area of control to another, the control responsibility is transferred. Each controller hands you on to another controller, like the baton in the relay race I described earlier. Across state or international borders, the service is the same for the same reason: to make air travel safe.

A Stressful Job

Why air traffic control is stressful is hard to define. There are deadlines, but because the situation's always changing, the deadlines to complete tasks change often. There are many things to do and only a certain amount of time to do them. Then there are all the rules and regulations you must comply with—you can't just do what you want. That's the general pressure that air traffic controllers feel. Further, sometimes the stress level increases due to a specific problem, anything from a mechanical failure to a passenger with a heart attack. When you think of all the millions of people who fly around the world, it's obvious that sooner or later, there's going to be someone having a heart attack or suddenly getting ill, and when that happens, that aircraft gets priority in scheduling.

We have a sequence of airplanes set up to arrive at the airport, and when one airplane says, "Hey, I don't want to be airplane number twenty-three, I want to be number one!" that causes us some problems. We have to juggle all the other aircraft to get this problem aircraft into the airport as quickly as possible. You only have a certain amount of room to play with, and sometimes there are more aircraft than you can handle comfortably. Unlike a traffic police officer, you can't say, "Stop!" although sometimes you'd like to. You just have to work as hard as you can to fix the problem and then sort out all the other aircraft. Meanwhile, the planes are all flying around in the terminal area at speeds from 100 to 300 miles (160 to 480 kilometers) per hour. They're always moving, so you can't pick a spot and say, "Stop there!" because they require a certain amount of room to maneuver. That's where the job becomes stressful, as you try to juggle everything around, create a spot for the priority aircraft, and keep up with everybody else at the same time.

At other times, there doesn't need to be a problem for the job to be stressful. All it takes is being busy without any time to relax. Air traffic control involves nonstop talking, thinking, and planning. There are times you're so busy that you lose track of the time you've been working. It flies by — literally.

The Right Stuff

The aptitude testing for air traffic control includes a psychological evaluation and IQ tests designed to see how smart you are, how quickly and well you can cope with changing situations, and how well you can perform multiple unrelated tasks. Several other tests examine your spatial reasoning ability, your ability to imagine where objects are in three dimensions. These aptitude tests take about four hours to complete.

The thing that makes the work of air traffic control unique is its three-dimensionality. Rather than just working with a flat plan, you're dealing with aircraft that may be climbing or descending. The picture you're trying to imagine is constantly changing, and you need to be able to picture where all the aircraft are and where they will all be in a few minutes. Especially in the terminal area, it's like a game of three-dimensional chess — where the pieces are moving at speeds of 300 miles (480 kilometers) per hour! You don't have hours to think about a move. You have to think as you are moving the piece, and every move must be correct.

In Australia, our training program is divided among the three groups of controllers: tower, terminal area, and en route. Trainees are sent to a college in Melbourne, and training is thorough and demanding, with a lot of exams. You have to get a mark of at least 80 percent to pass an exam. If you get less, you have to pass a supplementary exam. Fail twice, and your career as an air traffic controller may be nipped in the bud. Part of the training is working in a simulator that is just like an actual air traffic control console. Specialist operators in the simulator take the roles of the pilots flying the aircraft or controllers located in another center or in the tower. This simulator training determines whether or not you are suitable as a controller. A unique combination of skills is required to be a controller, and you either have them or you don't. It's not the sort of job where mistakes can be tolerated.

Recurrent Training and Checks

Once you have your air traffic control license, it's only the beginning of a series of tests and recurrent training sessions. Like pilots, we are required to undergo a performance assessment every six months. We work in a team structure, with about twelve people in each team plus a team leader who is a senior controller. The team leader is responsible for carrying out performance assessments of the team members.

Like a driving test, the six-month assessment is a procedure in which a team leader watches and listens to everything you say and do while you're on the job. They watch how you process traffic and make sure you comply with all regulations. At the end of it, they write up a report and tell you the areas you need to improve. If you don't do well, they can suspend your rating, which means you can't work until you've undergone a period of remedial training and passed another assessment.

We also do refresher simulator training on how to respond to in-flight emergencies. When you are in the middle of handling the emergency situation in this training, it feels just as real as working with real aircraft. In these sessions, we'll be close to working at our peak capacities, then the leader will start throwing in emergencies, failures, and various tricky situations. You walk out of that simulator with a real headache!

Same Time, Same Language

Air traffic controllers and pilots all use a special time called "Universal Coordinated Time." All the clocks around the world tell the same time on this system, which makes it pretty simple. Pilots and controllers don't have to worry about different time zones or international date lines, as the time is always the same. If we didn't have a standard time, we'd spend a lot of time just calculating when aircraft were due to arrive. Instead, by using Universal Coordinated Time, we just work on the fact that the aircraft departed at a certain time, and we know straight away what time the aircraft will arrive at Sydney.

As for language, the international language of air traffic control is English. There are some countries where some pilots speak to the controllers in their native language, whether it's Russian, Dutch, or whatever. But for international operations worldwide, pilots must be able to speak and understand English. As you know, there are various standards of English, so at times it can be a bit difficult knowing what the pilot is asking for or to get a readback from the pilot. A readback is when we tell the pilot certain instructions and require that the pilot read them back to us to indicate that he or she has received and understood the instructions. Sometimes, you are stuck in a situation where you're going backwards and forwards to the same pilot, saying the same things and trying to get a readback that sounds right. If we're having language problems, instead of issuing a complex series of instructions in one radio transmission, we will make a number of transmissions, one for each part of the instruction. This is to ensure that there is no possibility of misunderstanding.

Equipment

Whenever the airlines make technical advancements, air traffic controllers have to catch up. In Australia, we're updating equipment that has been in use since the sixties and seventies. We've undergone two equipment upgrades in the last ten years, and still another major upgrade will be done in the next two years. This will place Australia at the leading edge of air traffic control technology and will enable us to provide a more efficient service to the airlines. Many other countries, including the United States, are in the process of making major upgrades of their equipment.

Most of the old technology still works just fine, though. Even though the pilots in the 747 are surrounded by millions of dollars' worth of computers, we check their position reports using a plastic slide rule. In some countries, such as the United States, they no longer use slide rules. But I can assure you that these plastic slide rules work just fine. In 1993, I was involved with the introduction of new routes and control techniques throughout the Southeast Asia and Pacific Ocean regions. One of the things that the pilots asked is how we calculated things like time of passing—the time when two aircraft traveling the same route but in opposite directions will fly over one another, with the required vertical separation. I told them, "Well, we've got a little fifty-cent plastic slide rule and a formula. We spin the slide rule and calculate the time that way." Pilots continually tell us, "It's amazing how often you'll tell us we'll pass at a certain time, then we look out the window, and that aircraft will go by right on time."

Safety at Busy Airports

If you're worried about busy airports, just look at an airport like O'Hare in Chicago, which has nearly 900,000 aircraft movements (landings and takeoffs) a year. Then ask yourself how many accidents you've heard about at O'Hare.

Some people will say, "Well, how about ten years ago . . ." and I'll say, "That was ten years ago! Since then, there have been nearly *nine million* aircraft movements and millions of people in and out of O'Hare without a problem." I would feel extremely safe flying into O'Hare or any of the other major airports. Sydney has about 278,000 movements a year, and our busiest day had more than 900 aircraft movements. We are the sixth busiest airport outside North America after London/Heathrow, Paris/Charles de Gaulle, Frankfurt, Amsterdam, and Copenhagen, according to statistics from the Airports Council International.

If you think of the millions of aircraft movements performed by major airlines every day at major airports around the world, there is a very small number of accidents. In Australia, for example, we've had no fatal accidents involving airline passenger jet aircraft. People often become concerned when flying into countries where they believe the standards of both pilot skill and air traffic control may be questionable. All I can say is that the aircraft, the pilots, and the air traffic control have to meet international standards. We don't have a list saying, "Don't fly into country X or country Y." There are countries where there have been more accidents, but no matter where you go, flying remains the safest way to travel. (See page 139 after this chapter for more information on how challenges are met at busy airports.)

Backups for Systems Failures

People started becoming more worried about air traffic control systems blackouts after a number of incidents—not accidents—in the United States in which the radar and radio communications systems failed. While these failures do cause problems, backup systems and procedures rectify those problems. If something fails, you select the backup system, and normally the problem is solved. When equipment fails and there is no backup, we just work around that failure. We use different radio frequencies or change our procedures.

For example, if my radio fails, I'll call another controller and say, "I've had a radio failure—can you get one of your aircraft to broadcast on the frequency I was using to alert everyone of the failure?" Then I'll coordinate with that controller to organize transferring all my aircraft onto another radio frequency. Controllers can't dial up different frequencies, as we only have certain ones available. The pilots, on the other hand, can dial up any frequency they like on their radios. So you can very quickly transfer aircraft from one frequency to another to get around failures.

Taking Breaks

In Sydney, we work shifts of seven and a half hours. We work on a particular control position for about two to two and a half hours, then have a break of about thirty minutes. There are always more controllers rostered for duty than there are positions to be filled, and this ensures that there are always people available to give you a break.

You probably know yourself that in various situations, you say, "I've had enough," and you just want to go out and have a quick walk around, a cup of coffee, or just an escape from the office for a while. Well, air traffic controllers are the same, only we don't have the luxury of being able to just get up and walk away. We have to wait until it's time for our break or ask our supervisor to arrange for somebody to come back early from his or her break. But very rarely do controllers flip out or go crazy at the console or anything like that. If you've had a problem, or if you've been involved in some sort of emergency, the supervisor normally organizes a break for you once the problem is fixed. This is done to give you some time to recover, then it's back into it again. Sometimes, depending on the severity of the situation, you might be told to take the rest of the day off. In any event, air traffic controllers are pretty close-knit, and everyone backs everyone else up. If somebody's got a problem, and there are eight or nine people working there, they will all do everything they can to help take the pressure off the colleague with a problem.

Sick Controllers

Right from the start of our training, we are told that if we feel bad, we shouldn't come to work. And we don't come to work with a hangover or taking antihistamines or other medications that might make us drowsy. In Australia, regulations actually impose penalties on us if we turn up at work feeling unwell or unable to perform our normal duties due to medication. That fine is about AUS $1,500 to $2,500 (US $975 to $1625).

Controllers realize that if we turn up at work and we're not 100 percent up to our abilities, the potential is there for something to go very wrong. Our employment awards have been negotiated so that sick leave is available on a single-day basis pretty much all the time. We can get counseled or sent to other medical practitioners if we start abusing it, but it's entrenched in us that if you don't feel good, don't come to work! Every time we turn up to work, we're playing with people's lives. We can't afford to come to work and not be 100 percent ready to work.

If I make a mistake, I'll have to live with it for the rest of my life.

The Relay, Start to Finish

I'm often asked how we know where everyone wants to fly and how they are controlled. First, all aircraft must file a flight plan to fly in controlled air space, and these flight plans provide the controllers with the basic information needed to control the flight. The easiest way to see exactly how air traffic control works is to follow a flight from the planning stage until it arrives at its destination.

Aircraft are identified in one of two ways. The first is by its registration, as with the identification of motor vehicles. Each aircraft's registration identifies the country of registration and the identity of the aircraft. For example, Australian planes carry the identifier "VH" before the rest of the registration letters and numbers, such as "VH-ABC." U.S. aircraft have registrations starting with "N." There is very little need to actually read these numbers from a distance, as we use the radio to ask the pilot for the number. All the letters are pronounced using a special word for each letter, which is known as the phonetic alphabet. This means that, instead of "A-B-C, turn left heading one-three-zero," we say, "Alpha, Bravo, Charlie, turn left heading one-three-zero."

The second method of identifying aircraft is with the airline names and flight numbers. This method is used for all airlines operating on international flights, and in some countries, on all airline flights. The registration or airline name and flight number is used to identify which aircraft is making a request or being issued with instructions. This is called the "call sign" of the aircraft.

The flight plan is lodged for the flight by either the airline or the pilot, and contains the following information: call sign and type of aircraft; the time the aircraft wishes to depart; the departure airport, route to be flown, altitude desired, and destination; the total time for the flight; and any other special information, such as alternate airports or amount of fuel available. This information is sent via computer to all the air traffic control centers and towers that will need the information. At the control centers, flight plans are processed, and the information that each controller needs is written or computer-printed onto their computer displays.

Here's how it works from the points of view of both the controller and the pilot. Let's say we are following Qantas Flight Two from Sydney to Melbourne, and the call sign of the aircraft is Qantas 2. The crew meets at a special pilot briefing area at Qantas, where its members are given the flight plan that has been prepared by the airline. They also receive detailed information on weather, along with any special information about navigation aids or airports. Then they go off to the aircraft. By this time, the flight plan has been sent to all the air traffic control centers, and the controllers now have all the information required to process the flight.

Once the pilots are on board the aircraft and the passengers are boarding, the pilots contact air traffic control on the radio and request their "airways clearance." This is a set of instructions for the pilots to follow after takeoff to establish the aircraft on the correct route. It also serves as a double check that both the pilots and controllers have the same information.

Once everyone is on board and the plane is ready to push back from the terminal, the pilots call the surface movement controller — remember, he or she is in charge of the taxiways — and request clearance to push back and start engines: "Sydney ground, Qantas 2, gate 21, request push-back and start clearance."

The surface movement controller assesses the surrounding traffic and then approves the request or issues instructions for the pilots to follow before pushing back. "Qantas 2, push-back and start approved, time 34." The "34" means that the controller is giving the aircraft the time, which is the number of minutes past each hour, so the pilots can check to make sure their clocks are set at the correct time.

Once the engines are started and the aircraft is ready to start taxiing to the runway, the pilots again must ask permission to start moving. "Qantas 2, request taxi clearance." The surface movement controller again assesses the traffic and issues instructions that will allow the aircraft to taxi from the terminal to the runway, such as "Qantas 2, clear to taxi. Take the first taxiway left, then second right. Hold short of Runway 16."

As the aircraft is taxiing toward the runway, a lot of other things are happening. The pilots are completing their checks to make sure all the aircraft systems are functioning correctly, and they lower the flaps to takeoff setting. The cabin attendants are giving cabin safety briefing for the passengers, and they also check to see that the doors are closed properly.

When the aircraft approaches the runway, the surface movement controller instructs the pilots to contact the aerodrome controller — who is in charge of the runways — and to report, "Tower, Qantas 2 ready." This means that all cockpit checks have been completed and the pilots are ready to take off.

Normally, several aircraft are waiting on the taxiways to depart. The aerodrome controller determines the order for departure, depending on when they called "ready" and where they are in the queue. As the aircraft in front of Qantas 2 departs, the aerodrome controller calls the departures controller on a special phone line and tells him or her that the next aircraft to depart will be Qantas 2. The departure radar controller then checks the clearance of the aircraft, and if necessary, amends that clearance to ensure separation from other traffic.

Once this coordination has been done, the aerodrome controller assesses the traffic situation and decides whether the gap between the arriving aircraft and departing aircraft is sufficient to allow for an aircraft to depart. This requires very good judgment. When there is sufficient distance between the arriving and departing aircraft, the controller issues takeoff clearance: "Qantas 2, cleared for takeoff. Contact Departures 129.7 airborne." The latter number refers to the radio frequency the pilots must use to call the departure radar controller.

The pilots acknowledge the takeoff clearance by saying, "Qantas 2 clear for takeoff." They then line up on the runway, increase the power on the engines, and away they go. Once airborne, they call the departures controller and say, "Departures, Qantas 2 left 700 feet on climb to 5000 feet." All jet aircraft departing from Sydney, for example, are given an initial clearance to climb to 5,000 feet (1,524 meters), which allows the controllers to efficiently utilize their airspace close to the airport.

The departures controller checks that the correct information is being displayed on his or her radar and then checks for any potential separation problems with other aircraft. Provided there are no potential problems, the aircraft is instructed to climb to the upper level of departures airspace. The departures controller says, "Qantas 2 identified, climb to flight level two-eight-zero." Above 10,000 feet (3,049 meters), the aircraft fly at altitudes called "flight levels." Flight level two-eight-zero is 28,000 feet (8,537 meters).

The departures controller then calls the Melbourne en route sector and tells them that Qantas 2 has departed and at what time. This information is subsequently passed to the Melbourne air traffic control tower.

Provided there are no separation problems, the aircraft flies, complying with the airways clearance and follows the flight-planned route to Melbourne. When the aircraft is about thirty miles (forty-eight kilometers) south of Sydney, the departures controller calls the Melbourne en route controller and hands off the radar identification of the aircraft and transfers the control and separation responsibility. This is the third baton change in the flight so far. (The first was the change from surface movement controller to aerodrome control; the second was aerodrome control to departures control.)

The departures controller then instructs Qantas 2 to call the Melbourne controller: "Qantas 2 contact Melbourne Center on 125.6." The aircraft then calls on the new frequency, and the Melbourne en route controller monitors its flight-planned route for any other aircraft that may cause a separation problem. The controller checks to see if the planned flight level is available and then clears the aircraft to climb. In this case, Qantas 2 has planned to cruise at flight level three-nine-zero, or an amended level may be issued to maintain separation. So the en route controller will instruct, "Qantas 2 climb to flight level three-nine-zero."

The Melbourne en route controller maintains control and separation responsibility until the aircraft is about 100 miles north of Melbourne and then hands the aircraft on to the next sector. By this time, the aircraft usually has commenced its descent. This sector is known as "arrivals." The arrivals controller is responsible for making sure that aircraft are spaced out so that the approach controller can maintain aircraft in an orderly sequence for landing. As you can imagine, it would be impossible to separate all the aircraft if ten or twenty of them arrived at the airport at the same time! To prevent this, the landing position of each aircraft is worked out by a separate controller, known as the "flow controller." His or her job is to work out the best order for aircraft to arrive in, and to make sure that controllers do not become overloaded.

The flow controller talks to the arrivals controller and issues instructions as to whether aircraft are to enter holding patterns or if they can proceed to the terminal area. Holding patterns are used when too many planes are trying to get into the same airport. Obviously we cannot stop aircraft, so we place them in holding patterns. Holding patterns are often referred to as "stacks" or being "stacked up." This is because the controllers stack aircraft up above one another in the holding pattern using vertical separation. Then, when there is room to start bringing aircraft out of the patterns, we start at the bottom of the stack and tell the lowest aircraft to stop holding and continue on to the airport. Then we slowly move up the stack until all of the airplanes are out of the holding pattern. It's just like dealing from the bottom of a deck of cards.

The arrivals controller hands off Qantas 2 to the Melbourne approach controller at thirty miles (forty-eight kilometers) north of Melbourne. The approach controller issues instructions to keep Qantas 2 descending and may also instruct the pilots to turn onto specific headings to position the aircraft for the runway. The planes fly different types of approaches, depending on whether it is cloudy or clear. The approach controller is aware of the weather conditions and positions Qantas 2 to intercept the center line of runway 27. Once the aircraft is established on final approach and inside about ten miles (sixteen kilometers) from touchdown, the pilots are told to call Melbourne Tower.

The subsequent exchange would go like this: "Melbourne Tower, Qantas 2 on final runway 27."

"Qantas 2 cleared to land runway 27."

Once the aircraft has landed and turned off the runway, the pilots call the surface movement controller for guidance to the terminal. Once the plane is stopped at the gate, its contact with air traffic control is at an end.

This same process is carried out around the world every day for thousands and thousands of flights of varying lengths.

Means of Separation

To control the traffic, we have regulations that require us to maintain separation between aircraft. An air traffic controller's methods of separation are the tools of his or her trade: They are radar, vertical separation, distance separation, and time separation. Each of these separation standards is used for different situations, and we choose the specific tool to do exactly the right job.

RADAR. The word "radar" stands for "radio direction and range." Radar was developed during World War II, primarily as an early warning system for enemy aircraft, then further refined to assist in the interception of enemy aircraft. It later became the most significant tool used by air traffic controllers.

Radar allows the controller to observe on a display the position and direction of flight of any aircraft within the range of the radar. Radar is very accurate and, with the advances in equipment technology both on the ground and in aircraft, controllers now receive information on both the speed and altitude of each plane. Radar can be located anywhere there is power to run the equipment. Within Australia, we have uninterrupted radar coverage along the entire East Coast, from 250 miles (400 kilometers) north of Cairns down to Tasmania and across to Adelaide. There are also radar sites located in Perth and Darwin, along with many military radar sites. Each radar system used in Australia has a range of 250 miles, and sites are located to provide overlapping coverage in case one site fails. The setup is similar in other countries. In the United States, hundreds of radar sites provide coverage for nearly the entire country.

On radar, the minimum spacing allowed between aircraft is between three and five miles, depending on the distance the aircraft is from the radar site and depending on the radar accuracy. I don't want to get too technical, but there are two types of radar information we can get. There are also different separation requirements depending on how many revolutions per minute the radar head does—whether you get an updated position every three seconds or every fifteen seconds and so on.

VERTICAL SEPARATION. Vertical separation means instructing aircraft to fly at different altitudes so that they are separated by a minimum vertical distance, measured in feet. By international agreement, the minimum separation varies depending on the height the aircraft are flying. For aircraft flying below 29,000 feet (8,700 meters), the minimum separation is 1,000 feet (300 meters) between aircraft. Above 29,000 feet, the minimum separation is usually 2,000 feet (600 meters) because of atmospheric differences. To enhance the safety of vertical separation, different altitudes are assigned depending on which way the aircraft is traveling. Aircraft heading to the west are assigned even-numbered levels below 29,000 feet—such as 6,000 or 8,000 feet (1,800 to 2,400 meters), for example—and those heading east are assigned levels in odd numerations.

Above 29,000 feet, the system varies, due to the separation of 2,000 feet required. Westbound aircraft are assigned levels from 31,000 feet (9,300 meters) in 4,000-foot (1,200-meter) increments—in other words, they fly at 31,000 feet, at 35,000 feet (10,500 meters), or at 39,000 feet (11,700 meters). Eastbound aircraft are assigned to 33,000, 37,000, and 41,000 feet (9,900, 11,000, and 12,300 meters), until a plane cannot accept higher levels. Most commercial jet aircraft operate between 28,000 and 41,000 feet (8,400 and 12,300 meters).

Recently in the North Atlantic area—the airspace between America and Europe where the majority of transcontinental flights operate—air traffic control has been using 1,000 feet of vertical separation at all levels to accommodate the high number of aircraft using this area. Yet the aircraft in these cases have to comply with an increased standard of altimetry (height-measuring) equipment.

DISTANCE SEPARATION; NAVIGATION. Distance separation is used in areas where there is no radar coverage, such as oceanic areas or areas over the middle of Australia with no suitable sites for radar. Aircraft use various navigation aids that allow controllers to establish accurately the distance an aircraft is from a specific point or navigation aid.

Controllers use two means to establish how far an aircraft is away from a certain point. One is Distance Measuring Equipment (DME), which is a radio beacon on the ground that the aircraft can tune into to get a readout of the distance to or from the beacon. The other method uses sophisticated onboard computer systems. These are inertial navigation systems/inertial reference systems (INS/IRS) and global positioning system (GPS), systems that are fitted to the majority of airline aircraft and used to calculate the exact position of the aircraft.

Inertial navigation systems were developed for use in guided missiles and the U.S. space program. A series of accelerometers measures the different forces acting on the aircraft and helps to determine the change in position of the aircraft. These systems require the pilot to accurately enter the latitude and longitude of the aircraft parking position before the aircraft starts to move. That parking position is contained in the pilot's documents and is often painted or displayed on the terminal.

Once the inertial system knows that particular point, it will be able to tell you how to get to another point as well as the distance to that point.

Global positioning systems are relatively new in commercial aircraft fleets, but they already have demonstrated incredible accuracy. The GPS was developed by the U.S. military to guide everything from aircraft to atom bombs. The GPS relies on a network of twenty-four satellites that send coded signals to a receiver. The computer inside the receiver is then able to calculate the exact position of the aircraft. The starting position of the aircraft doesn't need to be entered, because the system knows where it is as soon as it receives enough signals from the satellites to calculate its position. To receive a good position fix, the receiver needs signals from at least three satellites.

These systems provide the pilot with the exact position of the aircraft, the distance to any point on its route or any other point entered into the computer, and the time it will take at the present speed to reach that point. Controllers are most interested in these systems' ability to provide accurate estimates for the time an aircraft will reach points on the aircraft's route and the distance the aircraft is from that point or any other point specified.

Controllers ask the pilots to report how far the aircraft is from a certain point, and we then use that distance to establish separation from any other aircraft. The minimum distance allowed between aircraft being separated using this method varies from five miles to 80 miles (128 kilometers). The distance used depends on the aircraft, the ground equipment available, and where the aircraft is flying. Generally, most aircraft operate in areas where the minimum separation is twenty miles (thirty-two kilometers).

Distance separation is a bit like driving on a freeway—you leave a certain distance between yourself and the car in front of you. Controllers use distance separation to allow more than one aircraft to fly along the same route at the same level. The controllers know what speeds the aircraft are flying and constantly check the separation to ensure the minimum distance is not infringed upon.

The other form of distance separation used specifies a minimum distance between the routes the aircraft are flying. This standard is very important outside the area covered by radar. We know the route the aircraft has been cleared to fly along, and then we allow a tolerance of error on either side of the aircraft's route. Imagine that you're driving down a freeway with two lanes and instead of traveling either in the left lane or right lane, you actually travel along with the center line of the freeway going straight down the middle of your car. Well, that's what an aircraft does. It flies along a route with the center line going down the middle of the aircraft, so it has room on either side to allow for navigation tolerances of error.

We then ensure that the tolerances of error of each route do not overlap, just as a freeway is divided in the middle with a space between the two sets of lanes. From my experiences flying in the cockpit as an observer all over the Asia-Pacific region, aircraft using INS/IRS or GPS have incredibly small navigation tolerances of error—they are always right on the center line of their route.

TIME SEPARATION. Time separation is the other method of ensuring separation when aircraft are flying outside radar coverage and is used when distance separation is not available. As the name suggests, we ensure that a specified time exists between aircraft at the same level to ensure separation. Controllers have a number of different time standards that they can use, depending on the situation. The minimum time separation varies from one minute for aircraft departing from an airport up to twenty minutes for aircraft on long oceanic routes.

KEEPING CONGESTED AREAS SAFE:
THE AUTHOR INTERVIEWS
RON MORGAN,
FAA DIRECTOR OF AIR TRAFFIC

I have a friend in Manhattan—a dynamic, attractive woman who is a partner in a successful ad agency—whose fear of flying reaches a crescendo when she has to fly into and out of the airports around New York. In the skies where she imagines planes from Newark, JFK, La Guardia, and other airports to be vying for airspace, her mind roils with Dante-esque infernal imagery: overwhelmed air traffic controllers screaming with panic, equipment breaking down, and misguided planes colliding left and right.

It's for Judy and others like her, including my own nephew, that I spoke with Ron Morgan, director of air traffic for the Federal Aviation Administration in Washington, D.C., to find out why we should not be concerned about air traffic safety even when we're flying in and out of the most congested areas in the world. Morgan, who flies to about fifty cities a year in the United States and several abroad in the course of his job, says the only time he worries is when he's traveling in a car to or from the airport. "The U.S. has fifty percent of all air traffic control that occurs in the world," Morgan tells me. "When I speak to some of my colleagues overseas, it's hard for them to even imagine the volume of air

*The FAA's David J. Horley Air Traffic Control System Command Center
in Herndon, Virginia, about thirty miles west of Washington, D.C.,
is where the FAA, in cooperation with the airlines, manages the
flow of air traffic in the continental United States.*

traffic we have. But even with that volume, we still run the safest air
traffic control. Our system safely moves 1.6 million passengers a day
throughout the cities in the U.S."

Yes, Judy, it's true that the New York area is right up there as one
of the busiest areas for air traffic in the world. While Dallas/Forth Worth
International Airport may be the world's busiest single airport, with
935,000 air traffic movements (landings and takeoffs) in 1997,
according to FAA statistics, the New York area includes Newark
(467,000 in 1997); JFK (363,000); and La Guardia (354,000), not to
mention several smaller airports as well.

Yet the FAA's Morgan confidently and calmly lists the reasons why
we can be just as confident and calm flying into one of these airports as
anywhere else. They include the highly skilled air traffic controllers with
supplementary training for their busy areas; separate facilities to handle
combined airspace in areas where there are several airports; preset, strict
procedures for aircraft operating in these areas; sophisticated equipment
with backup systems in case primary systems should fail; and the Traffic
Collision Avoidance System required by the FAA on all larger commercial aircraft operating in the U.S.

"In congested areas, the air traffic controllers are highly skilled,

140

the most senior controllers in the country in both training and pay," Morgan says. These controllers are culled from the country's top-flight full-performance air traffic controllers and then given one to three years of additional training, depending on where they work, to learn to deal with a higher volume of air traffic and more complex configurations for approaches and departures.

Also, radar facilities look after all the planes in an area, not just for individual airports, and can see the "big picture." While each airport has its own air traffic control tower that is responsible for the planes on the ground at the airport, Morgan says, "When it gets into the terminal air traffic control radar aspect, we sometimes combine pieces of airspace so that one air traffic control facility handles the radar service to a number of airports. You really can't operate an independent facility for approach control for each one." In the New York area, for example, with La Guardia, JFK, Newark, and a number of smaller airports, all the planes in the area are handled by the New York Terminal Radar Approach Control facility, known as a TRACON, in Westbury, Long Island.

Morgan goes on to say that, in a large metropolitan area with lots of air traffic, air traffic controllers use a stricter set of procedures. "As a result, we have preset ways to handle any runway configurations for any airport or set of airports," he explains. "That tends to allow us to handle traffic much as you would with vehicular traffic in a metropolitan area, with one-way streets and left-hand turn lanes." An example of this would be a particular runway configuration for which all turns to final approach are left-hand turns, designed to avoid the air traffic of other airports that might be adjacent.

In addition to the skilled workforce and good procedures, the air traffic controllers at the busiest airports have a good set of equipment. "New equipment allows the controller to be more productive and assists him or her in decision making," Morgan explains. "There are certain things air traffic controllers do in the day-to-day job for which they use their brains, and these are variables best handled by humans. But especially in the radar department, automation can assist a controller and allow him or her to be more strategic and project further out with the number of variables. We call it 'decision support assistance.'" The reliability and not the age of all air traffic control equipment is key. "If it's available a hundred percent of the time, keep it," Morgan states. "If it's available ninety-eight percent of the time, replace it."

Yet even when systems fail, backup redundancy is built in, sometimes even third-level redundancy. "All of our critical equipment operates with backup capabilities and fail-safe systems," Morgan elaborates. "If the primary equipment fails, it automatically switches to the backup equipment. And in many of those systems, there's another level of redundancy in which a totally independent system can take over the job, should both primary and secondary systems fail. If *all* those systems were to fail, we have procedures in place to decrease the volume of aircraft in the area—never to decrease safety levels—so that the air traffic controller can do his or her job at a reduced volume of traffic."

Finally, there's a system that works independently of air traffic control and one that I was very relieved to hear about. That's the Traffic Collision Avoidance System, better known as TCAS (pronounced "tee-cass"). "In the U.S., if you have an airplane capable of flying with more than thirty passengers in commercial operations, you're required to have TCAS," Morgan says. "That pertains to U.S. flag carriers and international carriers operating in the U.S." TCAS gives the pilot on board a traffic picture immediately around the aircraft and gives the pilot "resolution advisories" in case another aircraft comes in close proximity. In other words, a voice message or pictorial message immediately advises the pilot what altitude to climb or descend to and at what rate. Adds Morgan, "If a resolution advisory involves two aircraft with TCAS, the equipment on board each aircraft coordinates the aircraft independently of pilots or air traffic control—by talking back and forth, the equipment provides the appropriate resolution advisory for both aircraft."

REPLACING FALSEHOODS WITH FACTS: DONALD EVANS'S STORY

The minute the plane starts to bounce, my heart rate goes off the charts. A feeling that is part anguish, part nausea, suffuses my entire physical self, right down to my fingertips—not nausea like I'm going to throw up but the exact same nausea I get when looking off a cliff.

—Judy Fayard
fearful flier, Paris, France

Donald Evans, having been too frightened to fly all his life, was in his late forties when he was finally coaxed to fly the few hours from Sydney to Adelaide in South Australia for the opportunity to be a judge at the Australian amateur waterskiing competition. The plane hadn't even left the ground when Evans's dread became something much more serious. "The flight attendants started showing us how to put on life jackets, and I was horrified," remembers Evans, now seventy. "I thought, obviously there is a chance this plane is going to crash!" In spite of the Valium Evans had taken to calm his nerves, every movement and noise the plane made and every encounter it had with a cloud became a source of terror for him. Even as the plane reached terra firma in Adelaide, Evans was a wreck, wondering if all the wheels had come out of the undercarriage.

Fortunately, help wasn't far away for the man who wanted to travel long distances only by cruise ship. A pharmacist in Sydney's eastern suburbs and a senior waterskiing judge for the state of New South Wales, Evans also has the distinction of being "Student One, Course One" in the Fearless Flyers course back in 1979.

Now about to plan a trip with his wife to Honolulu, the latest of many overseas flights he has made since recovering from fear of flying, the gentlemanly Evans is more than happy to tell me exactly what flying used to be like for him. Unable to sleep or drink or eat before the two round-trip plane trips he was able to make before he got help, Evans had a horror of being encased and enclosed in the plane. "I would break out in a cold sweat, and I just felt nervously unwell," he explains. Fear of heights took over once the plane left the ground, and Evans was unable to look out the window or believe that the plane was going to stay up in the sky. On top of that, he says, "Any noise—the wheels coming up, for example—made me want to jump out of my seat. A change of engine speed was frightening, because I'd think, 'Is the plane going to crash? Is it coming down?'"

Then there were the bumps. "Going into the clouds was terrifying because I thought the pilot wouldn't find a way out," he says. "Any change in weather or dark clouds, and I wanted to go and hide under my seat." Even the sight of flight attendants made Evans apprehensive rather than secure. "I thought, 'Why are they walking around looking at us? Is there something wrong?'" he recounts. In short, everything about flying left Evans paralyzed in his seat, unable even to venture to the toilet. "Even as we came down to land, my stomach felt as if it was in my mouth," he says.

It was with a vast sense of relief that Evans, less than a year after he had taken the second and last fear-filled flight of his life, opened the *Sydney Morning Herald* and spied a small ad announcing that a group of members of the Australian Women Pilots Association was starting a course for people who suffered from fear of flying. "I thought, at long last there was an opportunity to overcome my fear," he tells me. "I'm a positive sort of person, and if I make up my mind about something, it's extremely hard to shake me. So I approached the course with a positive feeling."

During the Fearless Flyers course, Evans had his misconceptions about air travel put to rest one by one. Having been convinced, for example, that the wings of an airplane were screwed on and would fall off if the plane hit some rough weather, he was reassured to hear that the wing was one solid piece. He got a lot of confidence from hearing the Qantas pilots and engineers who spoke to the class, and he welcomed the news that a four-engine plane would fly on one engine. He loved visiting the air traffic control tower at Sydney Airport, hearing about weather and learning how carefully maintained the jets are. Gradually, every aspect of flying became as heartening as it had once been appalling.

The day of the graduation flight from Sydney to Melbourne, Evans sat next to Fearless Flyers founder Glenda Philpott and felt calm and collected until the flight hit a bit of turbulence. "She told me, 'We told you it's not always smooth, and this is nothing,'" he relates. "She held my hand, and I believed her, and forgot all about it after that." Buoyant, Evans walked around the plane chatting with classmates, visited the cockpit to greet the flight crew, and even looked out the window as the plane landed.

A couple of months later, Evans and his wife flew round-trip from Sydney to Tasmania, Australia's southern island state. Emboldened, he began traveling overseas to destinations such as North America and the United Kingdom and got hooked. "It has opened up the world to me," he comments about the change in his life the Fearless Flyers course has brought about. "The course gave me enormous confidence and got rid of all the fears associated with flying."

The pharmacist has one more parting shot. "When you run into some really rough weather, don't take a Valium," he advises. "Just breathe in and out! Turbulence is not something to fear, it's just an unsettling episode."

THINGS THAT GO BUMP
IN THE FLIGHT

Any kind of noise I hear from the plane makes me
wonder whether the plane is in good shape.
I worry about things falling apart because the plane
hasn't had a rest between flights.

—Judy Lotas
fearful flier, New York City

THE AUTHOR INTERVIEWS
PAUL BLANCH,
QANTAS MANAGER FOR FLIGHT
ENGINEER TRAINING

For phobic fliers, airplane noises are a common trigger for panic. Since fearful fliers are usually expecting the worst anyway, the sounds emitted by the aircraft during the flight signal to them that their favorite calamitous scenario is beginning to unfold. The vibrations I felt as a 747 left the ground were frightening for me, for example, as were virtually any decelerations in the engines at any time, but especially during takeoff.

The idea that these noises actually mean that the plane is performing perfectly seems like a radical suggestion at first. Yet you can eventually make these sounds blend into the background if you first learn what they mean and, second, remind yourself of this information each time you take a flight and hear them.

"The noises you hear are a normal part of aircraft operations," affirms Paul Blanch, Qantas's manager for flight engineer training and a volunteer at Fearless Flyers, explaining that all the bumps, whines, and vibrations of flight should be reassuring rather than unnerving. "The more one becomes accustomed to flying, the less evident these noises are." Even after all his exposure to fearful fliers, Blanch was still a bit surprised at the length of the list that I gave him of noises that might make a nervous passenger panic. Here Blanch tells us what those noises *really* signify.

148

Thuds and bumps as the plane is being prepared for departure

All cargo and food is stored in pallets, or containers. During loading and unloading, the pallets are positioned on floor-mounted rollers in the cargo compartment. When they hit the stops inside the compartments, they give loud thumps. In the main cabin, all the food is generally loaded in containers, and when the catering loading staff lock the containers into the galley modules, they generally make quite a bit of noise.

Cessation of air noise in the cabin while the plane is still at the gate

Before the engines start, air noise in the cabin stops. Because air-conditioning units in most airplanes are below the main cabin floor, these units are switched off prior to engine start to provide additional pneumatics (air pressure) for the engine starters.

Whining noises under the floor before departure

The lower cargo doors that facilitate loading of the containers into the lower hold are electrically driven. During their operation, you can hear a whining, whirring noise, and in some cases, significant vibration can be felt through the cabin floor while these doors are operating, particularly if you are seated directly above them.

Lights blinking and bells sounding

Following engine start, the pilot or flight engineer transfers electrical power from the aircraft's auxiliary power unit (APU) or ground power cart (which provides electric power for the airplane when the engines or APU aren't running) to the aircraft's generators. This can cause blinking of cabin lighting and activation of the in-cabin call system and bells.

During taxi to the runway, thumps from the nose of the plane as well as whirring and vibrations elsewhere

While the plane is taxiing for takeoff, the nose wheels often contact taxiway center lighting, which causes loud thumps through the landing gear shock absorbers, called "oleos." In addition, the flight crew will check the flight controls and move the flaps to the takeoff position. These produce significant noise during operations—a bit like the cargo doors' whirring noises. Sometimes when crew members move the flight controls full left and full right, checking for freedom of movement and correct sense, you can feel the vibration as they reach their limits.

Roars and shudders as the plane prepares to take off

There is a major increase in engine noise as the pilot or flight engineer sets the thrust for takeoff. There also is a lot of vibration, particularly in the rear cabin. This is due to exhaust from the engines—we call it "jet wash"—striking the aft fuselage and tail plane. (The tail plane is the horizontal mini-set of wings that is the part of the tail from which the rudder sticks up.)

Vibrations and knocking sounds following liftoff

After takeoff, the pilot will retract the landing gear. During this procedure, the landing gear doors open, and the brakes are applied to the main gear wheels to stop their rotation while they are retracting. The landing gear moves up into the wheel wells, and the doors reclose. On some aircraft, the nose gear has friction braking ("snubbers") that acts directly against the tires, which in turn causes significant vibration throughout the aircraft.

Slamming sounds from the galleys inside the plane during takeoff

This shouldn't happen, but loose articles in the galley modules may sometimes move during liftoff. It's disconcerting but harmless.

Sudden reduction in noise after takeoff

The pilot may be required to make noticeable power reductions after the takeoff due to air traffic control altitude restrictions or for noise abatement.

Noises above passengers' heads in the 747's first-class or front section

In the 747, the flight deck is above the forward cabin. During flight, two main noises can be heard from the ceiling area of the forward cabin. First, the flight engineer's seat is electrically operated along fore and aft tracks and produces noise during repositioning. Also, the stabilizer trim system, which the pilot uses to keep the aircraft on its flight path, produces a whirring noise during operation. After takeoff, when the flaps are being retracted, the pilot uses this system extensively.

Increases or decreases in air noise in the cabin at cruising altitude

There are subtle changes in the level of air-conditioning noise as the air-conditioning demands change, depending on the cabin's cooling or heating needs.

Bells going off during the flight

These could be passenger call bells for cabin attendants or cabin interphone call bells. In a large aircraft, it is necessary to have a telephone system so that the technical aircrew and the cabin attendants can communicate during the flight.

Decrease or increase in engine noise in midflight

This would always be associated with a climb or descent. During cruise flight, as fuel is used and the aircraft becomes lighter, the pilot may ask for a higher, more efficient altitude. This conserves fuel; aircraft operated closer to their optimum altitude are more fuel-efficient and therefore more cost-efficient. Slight changes in air-conditioning and engine noise will be evident during these ascents.

Reduction of power and more changes in cabin air noises when the aircraft starts its final descent

As the aircraft descends, the pilot will reduce power significantly. Associated with that, there is a change in air noise as the "engine bleeds" change from low stage to high stage. An "engine bleed" is a device for taking air from the compressor of the engine to provide air to the aircraft pneumatic system for pressurization, air-conditioning, and ancillary equipment, such as hydraulic pumps or leading edge flaps. When the pilot pulls the thrust back to idle at "top of descent"—the point at which the aircraft starts its descent—the low-stage bleed air decreases, and it is necessary to switch to a higher pressure area on the compressor.

Whirring, whining noises on approach

These sounds are the result of the operation of the leading edge and trailing edge flaps on the wings, which are driven by hydraulic or pneumatic motors. The flaps are lowered to enable the aircraft to fly at lower speeds.

Vibrations and increases in air noise, then a thump before landing

This is the landing gear extending. The wheel well doors open, the landing gear extends, and some of these doors reclose. Air noise is more noticeable as the doors open.

A roar after the plane touches down

After touchdown, the pilot will put the engines into reverse thrust. During this operation, a mechanical device in the engine deflects the air flow forward to provide aerodynamic braking. This is used in conjunction with the wheel brakes and speed brakes.

TIPS TO KEEP IN MIND
WHEN FLYING

When you run into some really rough weather,
don't take a Valium, just breathe in and out!
Turbulence is not something to fear,
it's just an unsettling episode.

—Donald Evans
Fearless Flyers class of October 1979

A week before the graduation flight, Glenda Philpott and other volunteers at Fearless Flyers suggest a number of things to do to make flying more comfortable, physically as well as psychologically. Here is a list of those tips, along with some of my own.

- Keep your life simple before a flight, even if your boss is making you crazy and you feel as if you have a million "loose ends" to tie up before you leave. Don't try to do too much the day you leave, or even a few days before departure. You will have that much less of a stress buildup to deal with before you get on a plane.

- Get to the airport in plenty of time to avoid the added stress of rushing to make a flight.

- Get a morning flight if you can possibly arrange it. You'll be more refreshed. Also, if you're a fearful flier for whom flying at night is or was particularly unnerving, flying in the morning puts you one step ahead of the game.

- Have confidence in your choice of airline. Avoid cheapo flights and "discount" airlines if you feel that their safety standards may not be up to par. Ask around about different airlines and people's experiences with them.

- Remember that recovery from fear of flying is progressive. Fly as often as you can. Each time it will get better, until before you know it, you'll be looking forward to your next flight.

- Keep up your recovery maintenance level. Before and during your flights, read as much as you can about aviation or materials from a fear-of-flying course. Bring your relaxation tapes, bring this book, and don't let too much time go by between flights.

- Don't fly on an empty stomach. Food can calm you.
- Avoid alcohol and drugs before and during a flight. They will only serve as a Band-Aid for your condition and will do nothing to cure it or even help you deal with your emotions. Besides, think of it this way: In the unlikely event that the plane had to be evacuated, how much would it help if you're three sheets to the proverbial wind and can't unbuckle your seat belt? On a more serious note, be aware if you are a heavy drinker, this may be exacerbating your condition in the long run, not soothing it.
- Avoid coffee. It's a stimulant and can be dehydrating.
- You can snap yourself out of negative thoughts—literally. Put a rubber band around your wrist and snap it whenever the "horror movies" come on.
- If you're feeling a panic coming on after you've boarded the plane and haven't mastered the exercises to cope with it, for heaven's sake, tell someone about your feelings! Sharing the burden will help you alleviate your fears. Who cares if you get a weird glance from somebody? You'll probably never see these people again.

  If you turn to a flight attendant, don't expect them to have had special training in helping fearful fliers. Most have not. But the better ones can be very sympathetic and have the advantage of being able to tell you what the plane is doing and the source of the noise or movement that has set you off. Even the person next to you can be an unexpected source of comfort.

- Tell yourself it's okay to be afraid—you'll be surprised how helpful acceptance is in alleviating the burden of fear. Then do what you've learned to calm those fears.
- If something unexpected happens, such as an aborted takeoff or landing, do not be alarmed if there is no announcement from the cockpit. This means only that the crew is doing just what you would expect and want: paying attention to flying the plane safely. The captain will update the passengers as soon as possible.
- If you're in recovery from fear of flying, ask the flight attendant if he or she is aware of any fearful fliers aboard. Offer to speak with them and share your knowledge. It will be as good for you

as it is for them. If you're afraid, it may distract you so much to meet a kindred spirit that you may not notice that the plane has taken off. But remember to share feelings, not horror stories.

- Keep the focus on where you're going, not how you're getting there. Picture that island in the South Pacific, the streets of Paris, or your bedroom at home.

- Visit the flight deck! It's very reassuring to be up near the controls, talking to the people who are flying your plane and asking them questions. On some international flights, limited visits are permitted during the flight. Tell the flight attendant that you are a fearful flier or in recovery and ask if you can go to the cockpit when there is a convenient time. (I always flash my Fearless Flyers card.) FAA regulations prohibit in-flight visits on U.S. airlines, but most U.S. pilots welcome visitors before the plane leaves the gate or after it has arrived at its destination.

- If you see a news item about an airplane accident, resist what may feel like an overpowering urge and don't read it!

  However, if you are unable to resist, keep in mind a couple of important facts. The first is that the airline industry is proactive in matters of safety. Every time there is an incident, it uses information learned from that incident to help prevent anything like it happening again anywhere. The second is that airline accident investigations sometimes take months or years to complete and that instant conclusions drawn by the media may not be accurate.

- Go to the airport nearest your home or office and spend some time watching the planes take off and land. It's mesmerizing as well as therapeutic.

Tips for All Fliers, Fearful or Not

- If your feet and ankles look as if they belong to a bag person after a long flight, you may unwittingly be aiding and abetting your discomfort. Don't eat everything the flight attendants put in front of you, as it can help bring on the bloat. If you have one or more empty seats next to you, be sure your feet are elevated. Stay well hydrated, but don't drink carbonated beverages. Those gases expand in your stomach as the plane's altitude increases. Support stockings or socks can also help.

- Every so often, get up and take a walk around the cabin. It'll help you stretch and keep your circulation going.

- Besides drinking lots of water, try smoothing lots of moisturizer on your face to counteract the dehydrating effects of jet travel.

- "Alcohol is a killer," warned my Fearless Flyers instructors. It exacerbates jet lag for anyone. (By the way, it takes one day for every four hours of change in time to get over jet lag.)

- If you need help sleeping on a long flight, take only short-acting sleep aids. Ask the attendant for head rest cushions or buy an inflatable cushion to put around your neck.

- Get oriented to your destination by setting your watch to the local time at your destination.

- If you travel when you've got a bad cold, ear congestion can be a problem during takeoff and descent. Take decongestants before flying and chew or suck on candy to help yourself swallow frequently to relieve pressure on the ears. In cases of severe pain, ask a member of the crew for a special inhalator.

- Bring a set of comfortable or baggy clothes to put on once the flight is in progress, even if an airplane toilet makes a cramped changing room. You'll be more comfortable, and your good clothes will look fresh when you get off the plane, helping you feel fresher.

- Where you sit can affect the way you feel. Try to get a seat that is not in the center section of a large jet. Aisle seats are best because you won't have to climb over anyone. If you sit near the window, however, you'll have control of the blind, as someone in a Fearless Flyers class pointed out. If movement bothers you, don't get a seat near the tail end of the jet.

NEED A QUICK REFRESHER BEFORE FLYING?

*The fear lasted only until my mind fed what I'd
learned from the course back to me.*

—Debbie Seaman
Fearless Flyers class of April 1995

You're sitting on a flight preparing to depart. You might be a fledgling recovered fearful flier who hasn't quite mastered the breathing exercises yet. Or perhaps you've let too much time go by between flights and your recovery maintenance level is low. You haven't had time to review the parts of this book you would like to. Bottom line: You feel nervous about the flight.

Here is a short list of some of the most reassuring reminders about aviation safety that you can take in at a glance. Think of it as your own flight checklist and review it on the runway.

- If the plane has a sudden drop in altitude, it's important to remember that there is no such thing as an air pocket. The plane is always flying, never falling. Turbulence cannot break a plane up and cause it to fall out of the sky—unless you happen to be flying over an active volcano. (Your pilot wouldn't do that!) Keep your seat belt fastened, and you won't be hurt.

- Few, if any, professionals have to undergo as many checks and license renewals as commercial pilots. And several times a year, they climb into the simulator to practice emergency procedures; they have to perform to the satisfaction of the airlines, or else they're grounded until they do. Other professionals in the aviation industry who also need to be able to respond quickly to emergencies—such as air traffic controllers and flight attendants—also undergo recurrent training.

- A pilot is trained to take off expecting an engine to fail, even though they rarely do, so he or she is ready to take immediate action if this does happen. There's plenty of power in the remaining engine or engines for the plane to continue taking off safely if this does happen. That's why, for example, a two-engine plane gets into the air quickly and steeply—because each engine has enough power to carry the plane by itself.

- If a jet cuts back its power during a climb, it's not because it's going to drop out of the sky. It could be because air traffic control has directed it to stay at a certain altitude for a while or because of noise abatement for residential areas near the airport.

- Even in the almost impossible event of all four engines of a jumbo jet failing in midflight, the aircraft will glide. Ditto for other types of aircraft. The plane is not out of control, and the pilot can land the aircraft without power. Don't forget, too, that there is plenty of time for the pilot to restart the engines.

- Airplanes can land and take off safely in fog. Both aircraft and airports with frequent low visibility have sophisticated equipment to facilitate this. Even if *you* can't see much out the window, trust that the pilots know where they are and so does air traffic control.

- Every time an aircraft noise or vibration starts to set you off, remember that these noises are signs that the plane is functioning exactly the way it is supposed to. Start thinking of these sounds as normal, not abnormal.

- The aviation industry loves backup systems. If an important piece of equipment on an aircraft fails, there is at least one backup system to take over, often two. By the same token, if part of the air traffic control system fails, there are backups to backups to backups. And don't forget all the built-in alarms to tell pilots and controllers of a potential problem and how they can avoid it.

- Even if you are flying in or out of an airport with a high volume of air traffic and other large airports in the area, you should not be concerned. There are separate facilities to handle combined airspace for areas with several airports, and the controllers in these areas are the crème de la crème, culled from air traffic control centers from around that country. They have supplementary training to handle this traffic—as well as higher pay. There are also preset strict procedures for aircraft operating in these areas—and a lot of sophisticated equipment.

- A lightning strike will not affect a plane's ability to fly, and all passengers and crew are as safe from lightning in a plane as they are in a car.

- Whether you're experiencing stormy weather or an unexpectedly firm landing, keep in mind that the plane you're in has been through the wringer of endurance tests by the manufacturer. It's built to withstand far more abuse than it's going to get in the course of commercial passenger service.

- Pilots aren't just winging the plane off into the wild blue yonder. Each takeoff and landing is a precisely calculated mathematical operation, taking into account the exact weight of the plane, its speed, the length of the runway, wind, and the outside temperature.

- The doors of the plane cannot be opened during flight unless the cabin is depressurized. Nor can the windows be shattered, as they are made with special materials.

- Old planes can fly as well as new ones if properly maintained.

- Each plane, as well as each one of its parts, has a detailed maintenance record, and aircraft and their parts are regularly, scrupulously gone over with tender loving care by highly skilled technicians. The planes and their parts undergo a series of standard checks ranging from the preflight check in which the pilot and ground engineer walk around the plane to examine it to the big one that takes place every 25,000 flying hours, in which the plane is entirely taken apart and reassembled.

- The statistics are definitely on your side. Massachusetts Institute of Technology professor Arnold Barnett estimated recently that a passenger has one chance in eight million of being killed in a fatal air crash; indeed, you'd have to take one flight per day at random for 21,000 years before being killed in a plane crash.

APPENDICES

APPENDIX A
WHERE ELSE TO FIND HELP

There are many fear-of-flying clinics in the United States, Australia, and around the world. If you have access to the Internet, you can visit the Web sites listed below. You can also get home study materials or attend workshops that travel to different locations. All prices given are current as of spring 1998.

UNITED STATES

NORTHEAST

SOAR
Westport, Connecticut

SOAR (Seminars on Aeroanxiety Relief) was founded in 1981 by Captain Tom Bunn, a United Airlines pilot and licensed therapist. The course covers psychology, aviation, and practice, a step-by-step approach that helps participants learn to fly confidently. The SOAR process starts with materials to use at home, including audiotapes and booklets. Participants then work one-on-one with Bunn, using his method of aeroanxiety relief therapy. Follow-up support is available on the program's toll-free number. The cost of the program is US $390 but SOAR can also be completed without the therapy sessions for US $285.

> SOAR
> P.O. Box 747
> Westport, CT 06881
> (800) 332-7359
> www.fearofflying.com

Institute for Psychology of Air Travel
Boston, Massachusetts

The Institute for Psychology of Air Travel offers ten-week programs at Logan International Airport for US $375 and seminars of different formats in other areas of the country. The programs are run by Dr. Al Forgione, a clinical psychologist and the author of *Fearless Flying: The Complete Program for Relaxed Air Travel* (Houghton Mifflin, 1980), and include training in desensitization, relaxation, and nutrition. Students are supplied with Dr. Forgione's book and tapes on relaxation, coping with stress, and answers to questions frequently asked by fearful fliers. Individual therapy for air travel and other phobias is also available, with two courses available on a parked plane.

> Al Forgione
> Institute for Psychology of Air Travel
> 551 Boyleston St.
> Boston, MA 02116
> (617) 437-1811; fax (617) 846-7242
> http://www.ads-online.com/inspsyair
> inspsyairt@aol.com

Open Skies
Boston, Massachusetts

Open Skies offers weekend seminars for small groups in any city. They have been held most frequently in Boston, New York, Newark, Chicago, and Los Angeles. The program is run by Diana Ronell, who has a Ph.D. in psychology from Adelphi University on Long Island, New York, where she did her dissertation on fear of flying. Dr. Ronell worked at Long Island Jewish Hospital's phobia clinic, one of the first in the United States. Formerly with Pan American's fear-of-flying program, she founded Open Skies in 1980 and has continued her research on fear of flying as a clinical instructor at Harvard Medical School. Open Skies' group programs focus on cognitive restructuring; anxiety, panic, and phobias; breathing retraining; aviation and how planes fly, with visits from aviation professionals; visits to a parked plane; and general information about air travel. The cost is US $495 per person, not including the graduation flight. One-hour individual sessions are also available.

> Dr. Diana Ronell
> Open Skies   or P.O. Box 1072
> P.O. Box 8, MIT Branch   40 W. 66th St.
> Cambridge, MA 02139   New York, NY 10023
> (617) 491-1296   (212) 592-4020

Solutions: A Brief Therapy Center
Albany, New York

This program is directed by Richard Platt, Ph.D., a professional member of the Anxiety Disorders Association of America and the American Psychological Association, with the cooperation of US Airways. The program includes four two-hour classes at the Albany International Airport in which an airline captain addresses the group; the group tours the air traffic control tower with an FAA official; the group boards a stationary jet; and the leaders teach anxiety management tools. The cost is US $500, including the flight, reading materials, and an audiotape. Individual sessions are also available.

> Richard Platt, Ph.D.
> Solutions: A Brief Therapy Center
> 346 Quail St.
> Albany, NY 12208
> (518) 482-1721; fax (518) 482-2829

Fly Without Fear
New York, New York

Fly Without Fear is an ongoing support and education group for fearful fliers that offers weekly evening sessions at La Guardia Airport. The group was founded in 1969 by Nate Cott, who wanted to cure his own "flight fright," and now is run by his daughter, Carol Cott Gross, another former fearful flier. The cost is US $100 for three sessions and US $30 each for subsequent meetings. Most members attend four to six sessions—consecutive sessions are the most effective—and go on to an optional group graduation flight. The sessions include visits to stationary planes; training in anxiety reduction techniques; and talks by psychologists, pilots, and experts in air traffic control and jet maintenance. Fly Without Fear also offers a packet of self-help information and tapes, including a summary of airplane noises and their explanations and relaxation exercises, which can be an especially useful tool for people who can't attend the program.

> Carol Cott Gross
> Fly Without Fear
> 310 Madison Ave.
> New York, NY 10017
> (212) 697-7666 or (516) 368-4244

Fly with Confidence
Glenshaw, Pennsylvania

Fly with Confidence seminars are given periodically at airports on the East Coast. They are taught by Carol Stauffer, M.S.W., who for many years taught US Airway's fear-of-flying program, and Gary Arlington, a pilot with US Airways. The seminars consist of two eight-hour sessions, including a round-trip graduation flight. The cost is US $350, or US $495 if the graduation flight is included. Stauffer teaches participants how to relax their minds and bodies with a cognitive therapy called "thought stopping." Captain Arlington covers pilot and attendant training, flight operations, safety procedures, aerodynamics, weather, air traffic control, and jet maintenance. A Fly with Confidence workbook, relaxation training audiotape, and the book *Fly Without Fear*, which was coauthored by Stauffer, are included.

Carol Stauffer, M.S.W., or Gary Arlington
Fly with Confidence
P.O. Box 100
Glenshaw, PA 15116
(412) 366-8112; fax (412) 366-1152
http://www.flywithconfidence.simplenet.com

SOUTHEAST

Freedom from Fear of Flying
Coral Gables, Florida

Freedom from Fear of Flying gives seminars for a maximum of ten people in major cities across the U.S. The fee of US $400 includes preparatory audiotapes, a booklet of answers to seventy-five questions from fearful fliers, sessions on parked planes, and relaxation training. An optional "celebration flight" is also available. Capt. T. W. Cummings, a retired Pan Am pilot, started the program in 1975, and has run it since 1982 with his wife, Carmen, a psychotherapist and former flight attendant.

Freedom from Fear of Flying
2021 Country Club Prado
Coral Gables, Florida 33134
(305) 261-7042

MIDWEST

Anxiety and Agoraphobia Treatment Center
Northbrook, Illinois, and Kenosha, Wisconsin

A special program for fear of flying is available at the Anxiety and Agoraphobia Treatment Center, which has branches in Northbrook, Illinois, and Kenosha, Wisconsin. Individual sessions are US $90 each, sessions at the airport are US $100, and a group flight is US $100 per person, plus airfare. The group program is US $400 for five sessions, plus the cost of the graduation flight. A follow-up program includes a Fearless Flying Support Group and practice flights. The program includes cognitive behavioral techniques and education about flying. Participants learn how to manage their anxieties and increase their feelings of control. The principal staff members are Karen Lynn Cassiday, Ph.D., and Marleen Lorenz, R.N., M.A.

Anxiety and Agoraphobia Treatment Center
666 Dundee Rd.   or 10400 - 75th St., Suite 311
Northbrook, IL 60062   Kenosha, WI 53142
708-577-8809   (414) 942-0966

Freedom to Fly
St. Louis, Missouri

This workshop is run by Ronald Scott, Ph.D., and Barbara S. Latal, R.N., C.S. The program is typically scheduled in six sessions—the first five are weekly two-hour group meetings and the sixth is a graduation flight. The program costs US $350 plus tickets for the flight. The course covers subjects ranging from anxieties to airlines and includes cognitive and behavioral coping skills, such as guided imagery and desensitization, and "in vivo" desensitization, which involves gradually approaching anxiety-provoking stimuli, such as the airport and parked planes. The program also includes a session with a pilot.

Freedom to Fly
777 S. New Ballas Road
St. Louis, MO, 63141
Ronald Scott, Ph.D. (314) 997-8877, ArJay0349@aol.com
Barbara S. Latal, R.N., C.S. (314) 849-9841

Flight to Freedom
Dallas, Texas

Flight to Freedom is a program run by American Airlines pilot Michael McKenzie. These quarterly weekend seminars include instruction in coping and relaxation skills and education on aerodynamics, aircraft maintenance, crew training, weather, and air traffic control. There is a tour of a parked airplane, and the seminar concludes with a round-trip graduation flight. Seminars cost US $395, including the flight, a breakfast, and instructional materials. Flight to Freedom also offers an audiotape entitled "Fly Free," which covers all the information given in the seminars and comes with a workbook for taking notes and "flight cards" describing each stage of a flight.

Michael McKenzie
Flight to Freedom
2407 Crockett Ct.
Grapevine, TX 76051
(817) 424-5108; fax (817) 421-7361
F2Freedom@aol.com

Flight Without Fear
Denver, Colorado

Flight Without Fear, organized by the Colorado 99s, is one of the only fear-of-flying clinics in the U.S. that includes visits to flight simulators. Eight-week courses are offered in the fall and spring, and include relaxation training; systematic desensitization; education on aerodynamics, weather, and safety; and tours of the United Airlines training facilities, air traffic control, and a parked airplane. The cost is US $375, including a graduation flight.

> Flight Without Fear
> Colorado 99s
> 14437 West 32nd Ave.
> Golden, CO 80401
> 303-780-5061

WEST COAST

The Fear of Flying Clinic
San Francisco, California

Fearless Flyers in Sydney is an offshoot of this clinic, run at San Francisco International Airport since 1976 by Fran Grant and Jeanne McElhatton, members of the 99s, the international organization of women pilots. The cost is US $545, plus a graduation flight to a West Coast destination. Using the facilities of United Airlines and United employees as guest speakers, the course covers pilot training and aerodynamics; jet maintenance; training for flight attendants; air traffic control, weather, and turbulence; and cognitive restructuring and education for the fearful flyer, provided by a behavioral psychologist. Courses can be arranged in other cities for a minimum of five people, at a higher cost.

> The Fear of Flying Clinic
> 1777 Borel Place #308
> San Mateo, CA 94002
> (650) 341-1595 or Fran Grant: (650) 345-2119
> www.fofc.com

Freedom to Fly
Woodland Hills, California

Freedom to Fly, founded in 1982 and based in Woodland Hills, California, is a six-session course run at Burbank Airport and Los Angeles International Airport by Dr. Ron Doctor, a clinical psychologist, author, and professor at California State University, Northridge. With a focus on psychology and development of skills for control of emotional reactions, the course includes tours of airport facilities, operations areas, and air traffic control centers as well as on-plane experiences such as talks with pilots and mechanics. The last session is the graduation flight. Freedom to Fly also offers an all-day course. The all-day sessions cost $135, and the six-session course costs US $325 plus the flight.

Dr. Ron Doctor
Freedom to Fly
5301 Commercio Lane
Woodland Hills, CA 91364
(818) 347-0191

Thairapy
Newport Beach, California

Thairapy offers one-day seminars at different locations around Southern California and has been operated since 1978 by Dr. Glen Arnold, a psychologist and licensed pilot specializing in aviation psychology. The seminars cover deep relaxation, cognitive therapy, nutrition, and aircraft operations, and can be held in any location. The cost is US $169. There is also a one-day flight simulator workshop that combines classroom teaching with a one-hour flight in a Boeing 727 flight simulator, in which participants take turns "flying" the simulator to get help with control problems and to experience simulated flight. This workshop costs US $289. Individual therapy is available for $120 per session and an audiocassette flight kit can be ordered for US $30.

Dr. Glen Arnold
Thairapy
4500 Campus Drive, Suite 628F
Newport Beach, CA 92660-1830
(714) 756-1133; fax (805) 722-9133

Fear of Flying Clinic
Seattle, Washington

The Fear of Flying Clinic in San Mateo, California, has a sister program in Seattle.

Fear of Flying Clinic
15127 Northeast 24th #211
Redmond, WA 98052
(206) 772-1122

SOUTHWEST

Dr. John Moran's Fear of Flying Class
Phoenix, Arizona

John Moran, Ph.D., offers an hour-and-a-half class for fearful fliers every other month in Terminal Three of Sky Harbor Airport. The first hour is spent in teaching exercises, and the last half hour is spent aboard a parked aircraft practicing anxiety control techniques. Each class is US $20.

> Dr. John Moran
> 7426 East Camelback Road
> Scottsdale, AZ 85251
> (602) 946-0801

OUTSIDE THE UNITED STATES

Fearless Flyers
Sydney, New South Wales

Schedules for Fearless Flyers in Sydney, the program on which this book is based, may be obtained by contacting Glenda Philpott. The cost is AUS $550 (US $357), including the graduation flight and lunch.

> Glenda Philpott
> Fearless Flyers
> P.O. Box 102
> Miranda NSW 2228 Australia
> (61-2) 9522-8455; fax (61-2) 9522-6541
> glendaph@zip.com.au

In the Melbourne area, the same program is offered in a course called the Fear of Flying Clinic. The cost is AUS $590 (US $383).

> Sue Litchfield
> Fear of Flying Clinic
> (No mailing address available)
> (61-2) 9439-9736; fax: (61-2) 9439-9736

Fearless Flyers is also available in Canberra in Australian Capital Territory, where the cost is also AUS $590 (US $383).

> Elisabeth Apps
> Fearless Flyers
> P.O. Box 7014, Mail Centre
> Canberra ACT 2610 Australia
> (61-2) 6231-3867; fax (61-2) 6296-3067

Austrian Airlines Fear of Flying Course
Vienna, Austria

Austrian Airlines in Vienna has offered fear-of-flying courses since 1980 by psychologist Dr. Robert Wolfger. The three-day seminar for groups up to fifteen includes an Austrian Airlines flight to a European capital. The class covers the roots and causes of fear of flying, breathing and relaxation exercises, aviation education, a visit to the Austrian Air Traffic Control Center, a discussion with air traffic controllers, a lesson on cockpit functions, and desensitization in a parked plane. The cost is ATS 4.900 (US $395), including the flight and the literature accompanying the course.

> Dr. Robert Wolfger
> Austrian Airlines
> Fontanstrasse 1
> A-1107 Vienna, Austria
> (43-1) 1766 2301; fax (43-1) 688-5501
> robert.wolfger@aua.com

S'Envoler de Preference avec Plaisir
Preferred Flying with Pleasure
Brussels, Belgium

Sabena Airlines sponsors two-day weekend seminars for fearful fliers in French and Dutch at Sabena House at Brussels National Airport. The seminars, which have an emphasis on training with a psychologist, include airplane visits and meetings with pilots and flight attendants during which participants have the opportunity to ask questions. The course ends with a round-trip flight, followed by a debriefing. Cost is 17,990 FB (US $485), which includes the flight and lunch both days.

> Sabena SA
> Capt. Pierre de Broqueville
> c/o Nadine Van Kerckhoven
> Sabena House Box 15
> B 1930 Zaventem, Belgium
> (32 2) 723-8792; fax (32 2) 723-8288

Up and Away
Toronto, Ontario

Up and Away offers five group sessions at Toronto's airport, conducted by Paul Griesbach, a behavioral therapist, and Diane Webb, a former fearful flier, in partnership with Canadian Airlines. The program addresses the most common causes of fear of flying, fear of impending disaster and anxiety about loss of control, and then uses behavior therapy such as relaxation training, thought stopping, and cognitive restructuring to understand and challenge these phobias. In each session, course members board an actual aircraft for cabin familiarization and discussions with airline captains on safety and crew training. The course concludes with a graduation flight. The cost of the program is Can $475 (US $330), including the graduation flight.

> Diane Webb
> Up and Away
> 2269 Lakeshore Blvd. West, Suite 2103
> Etobicoke, Ontario
> M8V 3X6 Canada
> (416) 503-3355; fax (416) 503-9995

Paul Griesbach's Behavior Therapy Institute also offers individual therapy for fear of flying. One-hour sessions cost Can $75 (US $52).

> Behavior Therapy Institute
> 62 Charles St. East
> Toronto, Ontario
> M4Y ITI Canada
> (416) 928-0858; fax (416) 928-0092

Seminars for Relaxed Flying
Munich, Germany

Argentur Texter-Millott, a group of psychologists in Germany, have been running their Seminars for Relaxed Flying in cooperation with Lufthansa since 1981. The seminars are held on weekends in Germany, London, Belgium, Spain, Luxembourg, and Italy. The weekend seminars cover the psychology of fear of flying, relaxation training and coping skills, a presentation of technical information by a Lufthansa pilot, and a graduation flight. The cost is GM 1100 (US $623), including the graduation flight. In-depth programs for individuals are also available. The seminars were conceived by psychologist Rudolph Kreftling, whose book *Relaxed Flying* was published in 1993 in German.

> Argentur Texter-Millott
> Hohenstaufenstrasse 1
> 80801 Munchen, Germany
> (49) 89 39 17 39; fax (49) 89 33 60 04
> argentur-texter@t-online.de

For seminars in London with this company, contact

Lufthansa German Airlines
Press and Public Relations
Lufthansa House, 10, Old Bond St.
London W1X 4EN
England
(44-181) 750-3415; fax (44-181) 750-3460

Freedom to Fly
London, England

The Freedom to Fly program in London offers two-session courses for groups of up to four people, run by Elaine Iljon Foreman, a clinical psychologist. Individual therapy is also available. The first session is a cognitive behavior therapy program tailored to the client's specific difficulties and the second part is a graduation flight with Foreman. The cost is £479 (US $795) per person, including the flight and meals. Individual sessions are available on request.

Elaine Iljon Foreman
EIF Consulting Rooms
21A Dean Road
London NW2 5AB
United Kingdom
(44-181) 459-3428; fax (44-181) 459-3428
free2fly@dial.pipex.com

For information on other London groups, see the Argentur Texter-Millott/Lufthansa listing in the Germany section.

Apprivoiser l'Avion (Taming the Airplane)
Paris, France

Apprivoiser l'Avion, coordinated by psychologist and fear of flying specialist Marie-Claude Dentan and supported by Air France, is held on an ongoing basis at Charles de Gaulle Airport in Roissy outside Paris. For groups of six people or less, the course includes an analysis of fear of flying and strategies for recovery; airplane familiarization; talks by and Q&A periods with an Air France captain and flight crew; and a half-day session in a flight simulator. Cost is 2,500 French francs (US $415).

Marie-Claude Dentan
Centre Anti-Stress Aéronautique
Air France
1 avenue du Maréchal Devaux
91551 Paray-Vieille-Poste Cédex France
(33 1) 41 75 15 41; fax 41 75 16 44

Fearless Flying Programmes
Dublin, Ireland

At the Dublin Airport, Aer Lingus Fearless Flying Programmes are run by Dr. Maeve Byrne-Crangle, psychologist and former Aer Lingus flight attendant. The basic program, which costs £346 pounds (US $574), includes ten one-hour sessions over five weeks, including a graduation flight. Other programs include a one-day program, an introductory program and graduation flight, and individual sessions.

Dr. Maeve Byrne-Crangle
Personnel Building
PA1, Aer Lingus
Dublin Airport
Dublin, Ireland
(353-1) 705-6983 or (353-1) 705-3200; fax (353-1) 705-3908

Norwegian Treatment Program for Flight Phobia
Oslo, Norway

The Norwegian Treatment Program for Flight Phobia is run by Professor Øivind Ekeberg of the University of Oslo in Norway with the Norwegian airline Braathens. The price is NKr 3,500 (US $475) and includes the ticket for the graduation flight and a book in Norwegian by Dr. Ekeberg on the treatment of flight phobia. The basic treatment principle is cognitive/behavioral, with a focus on aviation information, physical and psychological coping skills, and group sessions in which participants share concerns and try to help each other. The program also includes a film about flying, a visit to a simulator and an air traffic control tower, talks by airline pilots and flight attendants, education on topics from psychology to onboard equipment, and a graduation flight. Øivind Ekeberg, a medical doctor and university professor, has written numerous articles on the treatment of flight phobia.

Professor Øivind Ekeberg
Department of Behavioural Sciences in Medicine
Box 1111, Blindern   or Ingerid Seeberg
University of Oslo, Norway   Braathens, 1330
(47) 22 85 10 20   Oslo Lufthavn, Norway
oeekeber@online. no   (47) 67-59-70-00

AviaSafe
Stockholm, Sweden

AviaSafe offers three-day fear-of-flying seminars in cooperation with SAS Scandinavian Airlines. The company was founded in 1983 and is run by aviation psychologist Bengt Bylander with retired flight attendant Mall Yams. A flight instructor at the SAS Flight Academy, Bylander gives seminar participants access to the airline's MD-80 flight simulator and an emergency cabin mock-up for relaxation training. The course offers education on aerodynamics, aircraft maintenance and inspection, flight regulations, and safety statistics, and includes a visit to an SAS maintenance hangar and a demonstration at the air traffic control tower at Arlanda Airport in Stockholm, a graduation flight, and subsequent debriefing. The SAS Flight Academy donates the fares for the graduation flights as well as lunches and tea breaks. The seminar fee is SKr 8.100 (US $1,070), which includes a booklet and an audiotape.

Bengt Bylander
AviaSafe
Skolbacken 15
193 30 Sigtuna, Sweden
(46-8) 592-50598; fax (46-8) 592-50598

S'envoler sans S'affoler
(Fly Away Without Fear)
Geneva, Switzerland

The S'envoler sans S'affoler course, supported by Swissair, is given eight times a year at Geneva International Airport and lasts from Wednesday to Saturday morning. The cost is 750 Swiss Francs (US $504), including a graduation flight. The course is given in French, but if the participant has a basic knowledge of French, coordinator Fabienne Regard can help him or her in English, German, Spanish, Hebrew, and Russian. Each course is small (about six participants) and includes cognitive behavioral therapy; talks with a Swissair pilot and flight attendant; and instruction in exercises designed to help people manage their fears, initially on parked airplanes and finally on a graduation flight. (The flight at the end is not compulsory but highly recommended.) S'envoler sans S'affoler claims a 98 percent success rate and, as a follow-up to the course, an association of former participants organizes regular trips and meetings.

> S'envoler sans S'affoler
> Fabienne Regard
> 77 Rte du Chablais
> 74140 Veigy, France
> (33 4) 50 94 80 97
> Fregard@internet-Montblanc.fr
> Or call Cornelia Simeon at Swissair in Geneva
> (41 22) 799-3359

HOME STUDY

Courses that offer home study materials include Thairapy, SOAR, the Institute for the Psychology of Air Travel, Fly Without Fear, and Flight to Freedom.

TRAVELING COURSES

Courses that travel to other cities besides the ones in which they are based include the California Fear of Flying Clinic, Thairapy, Freedom from Fear of Flying, Institute for the Psychology of Air Travel, Open Skies, Fly with Confidence, and Seminars for Relaxed Flying.

WEB SITES

SOAR: www.fearofflying.com

Fly with Confidence: www.flywithconfidence.simplenet.com

Fear of Flying Clinic: www.fofc.com

Institute for the Psychology of Air Travel: www.ads-online.com/inspsyair

Federal Aviation Administration: www.faa.gov

The Boeing Company: www.boeing.com

APPENDIX B
YOUR PERSONAL RECOVERY LOG

It's crucial to remember that recovery from fear of flying gets better with time, practice, and work on your part. As you embark on the initial flights of your recovery, take this book along not only to review whatever sections you need to bolster your confidence but to record in this section observations about how you're getting better and what you need to improve. If you are painstaking about your recovery, each flight will get better until you might just be excited about flying. Bon voyage!

DATE:_____ AIRLINE/FLIGHT #:_____

FROM:_____ TO:_____

HOW FLIGHT WAS:_____

_____

WHAT RELAXATION EXERCISES I DID, WHEN:_____

_____

HOW I'M IMPROVING:_____

_____

WHAT THOUGHTS OR TECHNIQUES HELPED MOST:_____

_____

WHAT STILL NEEDS WORK:_____

_____

WHAT I MIGHT DO TO WORK AT IT:_____

_____

REMEMBER, IT TAKES TIME!

DATE:_____ AIRLINE/FLIGHT #:_____

FROM: _____ TO:_____

HOW FLIGHT WAS:_____

_____

_____

_____

WHAT RELAXATION EXERCISES I DID, WHEN:_____

_____

_____

_____

HOW I'M IMPROVING:_____

_____

_____

_____

WHAT THOUGHTS OR TECHNIQUES HELPED MOST:_____

_____

_____

_____

WHAT STILL NEEDS WORK:_____

_____

_____

_____

WHAT I MIGHT DO TO WORK AT IT:_____

_____

_____

_____

REMEMBER, IT TAKES TIME!

DATE:_____ AIRLINE/FLIGHT #:_____

FROM: _____ TO:_____

HOW FLIGHT WAS:_____

_____

_____

_____

WHAT RELAXATION EXERCISES I DID, WHEN:_____

_____

_____

_____

HOW I'M IMPROVING:_____

_____

_____

_____

WHAT THOUGHTS OR TECHNIQUES HELPED MOST:_____

_____

_____

_____

WHAT STILL NEEDS WORK:_____

_____

_____

_____

WHAT I MIGHT DO TO WORK AT IT:_____

_____

_____

_____

REMEMBER, IT TAKES TIME!

DATE:_____ AIRLINE/FLIGHT #:_____

FROM: _____ TO:_____

HOW FLIGHT WAS:_____

_____

_____

_____

WHAT RELAXATION EXERCISES I DID, WHEN:_____

_____

_____

_____

HOW I'M IMPROVING:_____

_____

_____

_____

WHAT THOUGHTS OR TECHNIQUES HELPED MOST:_____

_____

_____

_____

WHAT STILL NEEDS WORK:_____

_____

_____

_____

WHAT I MIGHT DO TO WORK AT IT:_____

_____

_____

_____

REMEMBER, IT TAKES TIME!

DATE:_____ AIRLINE/FLIGHT #:_____

FROM: _____ TO:_____

HOW FLIGHT WAS:_____

_____

_____

_____

WHAT RELAXATION EXERCISES I DID, WHEN:_____

_____

_____

_____

HOW I'M IMPROVING:_____

_____

_____

_____

WHAT THOUGHTS OR TECHNIQUES HELPED MOST:_____

_____

_____

_____

WHAT STILL NEEDS WORK:_____

_____

_____

_____

WHAT I MIGHT DO TO WORK AT IT:_____

_____

_____

_____

REMEMBER, IT TAKES TIME!

APPENDIX C
MAKE YOUR OWN RELAXATION TAPE

You can practice your relaxation techniques by going out and buying tapes designed for this purpose. But better still, you can use this transcript of the relaxation tape that Dr. Bryan Burke provides for Fearless Flyers students to make your own relaxation tapes. Ask the most relaxed person you know and trust, whether a friend or a member of your family, to record this onto a cassette. Alternatively, you can record it yourself. Use the tape regularly at home whenever you can get some time to yourself—preferably not right before bed, or you may fall asleep!—and take it on the plane when you travel. Eventually you won't need to rely on the tape to relax.

One more note: These relaxation techniques are useful for stress management in general, not just for fear of flying!

Fearless Flyers Clinic Relaxation Tape

Bryan Burke, counseling psychologist, welcomes you to this session of the Fearless Flyers Relaxation Tape.

If you are going to overcome your fear of flying, the fundamental thing you have to accept is that you are not a helpless victim. You must realize that you can affect how you feel in situations by being active and doing constructive things that help you stay in control. Instead of worrying yourself sick and psyching yourself out by doing things that undermine your confidence, you can reduce your fear of flying by

- Changing inaccurate beliefs that you hold on to
- Increasing your knowledge about aviation and flying
- Learning to relax

In this session, I am going to help you learn how to relax. You will do this using both physical and mental relaxation techniques.

Let's talk a little about relaxation. First, I want you to remember that relaxation is a natural bodily function. It's every bit as natural as panicking—something that people who tend to panic and terrorize themselves tend to forget. It's easy to believe that panic is basic to our nature and that relaxation is out of our control. But in reality, if you can do one, you can do the other.

Often people who terrorize themselves forget that a person cannot experience panic and be simultaneously relaxed. You either feel one or the other. By learning to relax, you automatically learn a way to control your panic. Progressive relaxation has a powerful effect on the body, including a reduction in pulse rate and blood pressure as well as a decrease in perspiration and respiration rates.

If you cannot relax naturally, then paradoxically, you have to work at relaxing. It isn't sufficient to say to yourself, "Relax," "Cool it," or "Take it easy." When we are wound up, we have to be active rather than passive, directing our body and our mind so that we start to feel different. We need to smooth the muscles and tissues of our body and refocus our mind onto calming thoughts and ideas, so that we become more peaceful and relaxed.

It's important to realize that people relax bit by bit, progressively—there's no need to hurry and no need to worry.

You can't do it wrong. You will relax at whatever rate you choose for your own body and your own mind.

Now let's start with our first relaxation training session. I want you to find a comfortable spot, somewhere quiet, away from interruptions like the telephone, children, and other distractions. Lie down facing the ceiling.

Imagine a straight line running straight through your body, cutting it in half. Balance yourself on either side of this imaginary line. Place your hands by your sides but not touching them, with palms of the hands facing upwards. Make yourself comfortable and feel your body pressing into the surface underneath you. Now close your eyes.

BREATHING. We will start by learning deep abdominal breathing. Slow, deep breathing is basic to the feeling of being relaxed.

If you are asleep or in a state of natural relaxation, your breathing is slow, deep, and easy. If by contrast you are aroused through excitement, fear, or other strong feelings, then your breathing is short, sharp, and shallow. In fact, changing your breathing pattern to slow, deep abdominal breathing will soon help you feel calmer and more relaxed.

Focus your attention on your breathing during this exercise. Do not become distracted by thoughts that come into your head. During this and other exercises, your mind may wander or you might become distracted. Gently pull yourself back, redirecting your thoughts to whatever you were practicing at the time.

Focus your attention on your breathing and listen to the sound of my voice.

Let your breathing become slower and slower . . . [Pause] . . . deeper and deeper. Don't strain, just slow your breathing down, easily and naturally. Inhale through your nose, filling your lungs like a big balloon, then hold it. Exhale through your open mouth, letting all the air out of your lungs, completely emptying the balloon . . . [Pause] . . . slower and deeper still.

Still slower, still deeper. As you breathe in, count silently under your breath "one–two–three–four–five." Then, as you breathe out, count "six–seven–eight–nine–ten." Take three or four deep breaths, counting silently to yourself to slow your breathing down, and filling your lungs with relaxing breath.

Remember, when you breathe out, it's important that all the air is breathed out. Keep on breathing out, pushing down on your chest, forcing the air out until all the air is exhaled.

Feeling calm, feeling heavy all over. Remember that slow, deep breathing alone can produce relaxation.

Try and maintain the deep breathing for the remainder of the exercises. You are teaching your body to relax and it is learning to respond to your wishes because you are in control. You can teach your body to relax, and it will respond. It does take practice and it does take time.

MUSCLE TENSION. The next step is to make sure you can really tell the difference between a tense muscle and a relaxed muscle. To do that, we'll tense and relax a few muscles.

Make a fist of your right hand. Squeeze it up . . . [Pause] . . . tighter . . . [Pause] . . . tighter . . . [Pause] . . . keep squeezing . . . [Pause] . . . tighter still. Feel that tension moving through your wrist, moving up the arm, and to the neck muscles. Just concentrate on that.

Relax now. Let your hand go limp. Start saying "Relax" each time you breathe out. Say "Relax" and let all the tensions go from your right hand. Be aware of the difference in feeling between your left and right hand.

Let's tense the left leg. Add tension to the left leg . . . [Pause] . . . tense . . . [Pause] . . . tight . . . [Pause] . . . hold it. Now let the tension go, loosening your left leg. Each time you breathe out, say the word "Relax."

Notice the difference in feeling between in your left and right legs.

PROGRESSIVE RELAXATION. Now I want you to lie in the same position with your eyes closed and just listen to my voice. I want you to progressively tense and relax the muscles in each part of your body in turn, starting from the feet and working up to your head. Although it may seem difficult at first, see if you can tighten just the muscle I mention . . . [Pause]. . . . This becomes easier with practice. Remember that all that's required is light tension—there's no need to strain. Also, if I ask you to tense a part of your body that is particularly sensitive, you know best whether to tense it or not.

Okay, concentrate all of your attention on your feet. Tighten the muscles in the toes and the arches of your two feet . . . [Pause]. Tighten them, tight . . . [Pause] . . . hold it, then let go, saying "Relax" as you breathe out, feeling calm . . . heavy . . . and more relaxed.

Now focus on the ankles and heels. Take a deep breath . . . then tighten the muscles in the ankles and heels . . . Tighten them, tight . . . hold it, then let go, saying "Relax" as you exhale through your open mouth, completely. Relax and take a deep breath. Inhale through your nose, filling your diaphragm like a balloon and exhaling through your open mouth, completely.

Now the calf muscles in your lower legs. Tighten those calf muscles . . . Tighten them, tight . . . hold it, then let go, saying "Relax" as you breathe out, feeling calm . . . heavy . . . and more relaxed.

And now the knees. See if you can tighten the muscles and connecting tissue in your knees . . . Tighten them . . . tight . . . hold it, then let go, saying "Relax" as you breathe out, feeling calm . . . heavy . . . and more relaxed.

And now your thighs. Think of the big muscles in your thighs . . . Tighten them, tight . . . hold it . . . then let go, saying "Relax" as you breathe out, feeling calm . . . heavy . . . and more relaxed.

Your buttocks and groin area. Be aware of the muscles in this area of your body . . . then tighten those muscles . . . Tighten them . . . tight . . . hold it, then let go, saying "Relax" as you breathe out, feeling calm . . . heavy . . . and more relaxed.

Now take a deep breath, inhaling through your nose, expanding your chest, and filling your lungs like a big stretched balloon, and hold it, then exhale through your open mouth, completely.

Now tighten all the muscles in your lower body . . . buttocks . . . groin . . . thighs . . . lower legs . . . and feet. All tight and tense . . . hold it . . . then relax. Feel the tension drain away as your muscles recover and return to rest.

Continue the deep breathing and focus your mind on your lower body. Concentrate your mind and let it wander through your lower body, checking out your muscles. If you find any tension or muscles still tight, smooth the tension away and tell the muscles to relax.

Now focus on the stomach. Is there a lot of tension there? We frequently hold a lot of tension in that part of our bodies. Think of your abdomen, tighten the muscles in your stomach. . . . Tighten them, tight . . . hold it . . . then let go, saying "Relax" as you breathe out, feeling calm . . . heavy . . . and more relaxed.

And then the chest. Focus attention on the muscles in the chest. . . . Tighten them, tight . . . hold it . . . then let go, saying "Relax" as you breathe out, feeling calm . . . heavy . . . and more relaxed.

Now think of the shoulders. We carry a lot of weight on our shoulders. Think of how much tension and pressure there is around your shoulders at the moment. Tighten the muscles in your shoulders. . . . Tighten them, tight . . . hold it, then let go, saying "Relax" as you breathe out, feeling calm . . . heavy . . . and more relaxed.

Focus now on your back. Tighten the muscles in your lower back, then your upper back . . . tighten . . . tighten them . . . tight . . . hold it, then let go, saying "Relax" as you breathe out, feeling calm . . . heavy . . . and more relaxed.

Now your upper arms. Concentrate on the muscles in the upper arms between the elbow and the shoulders. . . . Tighten them . . . tight . . . hold it, then let go, saying "Relax" as you breathe out, feeling calm . . . heavy . . . and more relaxed.

Now your lower arms. Concentrate on the muscles in the lower arms between the elbow and the hand. Tighten them . . . tight . . . hold it, then let go, saying "Relax" as you breathe out, feeling calm . . . heavy . . . and more relaxed.

Now your hands. Tighten the muscles in your hands and fingers. . . . Tighten them, tight . . . hold it, then let go, saying "Relax" as you breathe out, feeling calm . . . heavy . . . and more relaxed.

Now take a deep breath, inhaling through your nose, expanding your chest and filling your lungs like a big stretched balloon, and hold it, then exhale through your open mouth, completely.

Now tighten all the muscles in your upper body . . . stomach, chest, shoulders, lower back, arms, and hands . . . all tight and tense . . . hold it . . . then relax. Feel the tension drain away as your muscles recover and return to rest.

Continue the deep breathing and focus your mind on your upper body. Let your concentration wander through your upper body and check out your muscles. If you find any tension or muscles still tight, smooth the tension away and tell the muscles to relax.

Now the muscles of the neck. Tighten . . . hard . . . stiff . . . tighten them, tight . . . hold it, then let go, saying "Relax" as you breathe out, feeling calm . . . heavy . . . and more relaxed.

Now concentrate your attention on your face. Tighten the muscles in your chin . . . your lips . . . mouth . . . cheeks . . . eyes . . . forehead . . . scalp . . . all feeling tight . . . tighten those muscles. . . . Tighten them, tight . . . hold it, then let go, saying "Relax" as you breathe out, feeling calm . . . heavy . . . and more relaxed.

Let your eyes become heavy and let them fall back into your head . . . your forehead . . . and the top of your head. Say "Relax."

And you can feel all the strains, the pressures, and the tensions moving from your head . . . and you are feeling very relaxed. Your body feels very heavy, all the energy has drained out of it. You are feeling relaxed and at peace.

Continue the deep breathing and focus your mind on your body. Let your concentration wander over your body, checking out the muscles in your head and neck, upper body, lower body. If you find any tension or muscles still tight, smooth the tension away and tell the muscles to relax.

MENTAL RELAXATION. Another way to relax is to refocus your mind. The mind is like a television set with a broken on/off switch. All the time we are awake, there are thoughts in our minds. When we're watching TV and a program is upsetting us, we have to change the channel. In the same way, we have to refocus our mind on thoughts or images that are soothing, reassuring, and comforting.

All too often, we worry ourselves sick by continuing to think of unpleasant, negative things, of catastrophic outcomes. I call this obsessive-thinking self-sabotage, because it not only makes us feel bad but it undermines our ability to do something constructive about the thing or situation concerning us.

SAFE PLACE. I want you to imagine that you are in a very safe place. Let's say you are in a room that is special to you, a room in your present home or your childhood home. I want you to create this room in your mind— imagine the room . . . the shape and size of the room . . . the openings from doors and windows or skylights. If your mind wanders, as it often does, just gently say to yourself "Stop" and refocus on your safe place . . . see the furniture in the room . . . the ornaments and things on the walls . . . see the colors . . . be aware of the patterns of light from the windows or lamps in the room . . . feel the textures . . . experience the smells . . . hear the sounds that you associate with your safe place. Just imagine yourself in this room. You are feeling very relaxed and very comfortable and very safe. You feel very safe and totally relaxed in your safe place.

Just enjoy this feeling for a moment or two. Remember, if other thoughts intrude, just gently say "Stop" and bring your mind back to your safe place.

And now a lighted candle appears in your room. The flame dances and prances in front of you, capturing all your attention. That's all you can see, just a single candle and its flame. All else is out of your mind, and you are feeling very warm and at peace. Completely relaxed . . . and you are feeling very heavy . . . and your body is pressing into the floor, and you are warm and safe and in control. As you watch, the flame gets brighter . . . brighter and white . . . brighter and brighter still, until all you can see is a bright white haze. You are just floating, feeling relaxed and safe. Stay there for the next few minutes in your safe place, feeling calm . . . heavy . . . and very relaxed.

And now the light starts to change and the haze clears. Once again, you see a room, but this time it is the room you left behind. See the room and imagine what it looks like . . . the shape and size of the room . . . the doors and windows . . . furniture . . . colors . . . see yourself in the room . . . imagine what you will see when you open your eyes.

REENTRY. Now you're moving from that very safe spot. You're coming back to where you were at the beginning. You're taking a deeper breath, you can feel that energy coming into your body, you're beginning to wake up, and you can feel your body becoming alive. And you feel very, very relaxed.

Now I'm going to start counting backwards from five, and when I reach one, I want you to open your eyes and sit up very, very slowly.

Five . . . your eyes are getting lighter . . . . Four, lighter and lighter still. . . . Three, lighter, you can feel things around you. . . . Two, you're becoming aware of what's going on around you . . . and . . . one, your eyes just gently open and you return to the room you left behind.

You are sitting up slowly . . . very, very slowly . . . and you are fully aware of what is going on around about you, only you are very, very relaxed.

That was very good. This is the end of this session. Thank you!

APPENDIX D
CONTRIBUTORS

Some of the contributors to *The Fearless Flier's Handbook*, such as program leader Glenda Philpott and the course graduates whose stories are told in these pages, have personal information incorporated into their chapters. Here's a little more about some of the other contributors, in alphabetical order. To everyone who has made this book possible, I give my thanks and gratitude for your tremendous help and your infinite patience!

Ken Anderson

Ken Anderson began his career with Qantas in early 1963, when still in his teens, as an electrical engineer trainee. After four years, he earned a tradesperson's qualification and started a course on the Boeing 707 to be a licensed aircraft maintenance engineer, a position that allows you to "sign out" aircraft as being serviceable. But before that course was over, Qantas advertised for eight flight engineers and Anderson volunteered for the job, leaving electrical engineering behind. He finished the 707 course and then went directly into flight engineer training. He first flew in 1969, at the age of twenty-three.

In 1977, Anderson trained to become a senior check flight engineer, responsible for initial and recurrent training of Qantas flight engineers, Qantas junior pilots (who are licensed to provide in-flight relief for flight engineers), Australian Air Force personnel, and others who bought or leased Qantas 707s. Two and a half years later, he began to specialize in 747s and went back to working as a "line flight engineer" flying on Qantas routes. In 1989, he was wooed back to the training section as a senior check flight engineer. That is his current position.

Paul Blanch

Paul Blanch, the manager of flight engineer training for Qantas at the airline's jet base at Sydney Airport, started his career at Qantas in 1962 as an apprentice aircraft maintenance engineer. He joined the airline's flight operations department as a flight engineer six years later. In his current position, he is responsible for training pilot and flight engineer candidates on the Boeing 747 and for the recurrent training and license renewals for flight engineers and second officers. He also spends about a third of his work time in the air and has logged about 15,000 flying hours as a flight engineer.

One Tuesday evening in the early 1990s, Blanch was asked to speak to a Fearless Flyers class to fill in for a supervisor who couldn't make it. "I never left," he chuckles. He has lectured on different topics but usually can be found helping awed, recovering fearful fliers "fly" 747 simulators.

Like everyone who teaches at Fearless Flyers, Blanch loves flying. "I find it relaxing, challenging, and extremely satisfying," he tells me. "And I would love everybody to get as much enjoyment out of it as I do. That's why I lecture at the Fearless Flyers course, because fearful fliers are missing out on a great experience."

Bryan Burke

Dr. Bryan Burke is a psychologist, who counsels international students and runs the foreign exchange program at the University of New South Wales in Sydney, Australia. Burke is also the counselor for the Fearless Flyers clinic and has a private practice helping fearful fliers overcome their phobias. Since 1988, his measured, mellifluous tones have become familiar to the hundreds who have heard him speak at Fearless Flyers clinics, and have listened to his relaxation tapes during the course and during the flights that followed. The coping skills he teaches helps fearful fliers fly more comfortably and confidently by controlling their fears.

Alan Dukes

A terminal area full-performance controller—the title means that he is a senior controller monitoring planes in the air within a thirty- to forty-five-mile radius of the airport—Alan Dukes has been Fearless Flyers' air traffic control liaison since the mid-1980s. His partner in this endeavor is Tim Sercombe, who is a full-performance controller in the tower itself, overseeing planes on the ground and taking off or landing.

Dukes lives with his wife, Linda Sweet, and their two children near the Sydney airport, where he has been an air traffic controller since 1982.

Ken Dunkley

Ken Dunkley, who is Qantas's manager of mechanical systems engineering, has been sharing his knowledge of airplanes with fearful fliers since the early 1980s, sometimes spending hours of extra time tutoring the particularly terrified, right up to and including graduation flights.

Along with a pilot's license, Dunkley has a B.S. in aeronautical engineering from the University of New South Wales in Sydney and a graduate diploma in industrial engineering.

Dunkley is no stranger to raised pulses on airplanes. Before he joined Qantas as an aeronautical engineer in 1966, he worked for an organization that overhauled military airplanes. Geared up in helmet and oxygen mask, with legs strapped into an ejection seat, Dunkley frequently was sent along on test flights. When test pilots took up civil airplanes to get them certified in an aerobatic capacity—putting the planes through spins, in other words—Dunkley went along to keep a camera trained on the instruments panel.

At home, Dunkley spends a lot of time building award-winning model aircraft with his sons. He also participated in building a full-size replica of the first Qantas aircraft, which is on display at the Qantas Museum in Longreach, Queensland. That artistic streak is also evident in the poems he has penned in praise of flying and of the Fearless Flyers classes for their accomplishments.

Robert C. Fischer

Robert C. Fischer, who created the illustrations for *The Fearless Flier's Handbook*, spent twenty-five years as a creative director for advertising agencies in the U.S., Europe, and Latin America and currently resides in Manhattan. He credits his cartoon characters (or, as someone once described them, "the people in his bottom drawer") for easing the pressure of having to create hard-selling campaigns for clients such as Procter & Gamble, Mars M&Ms, Coca-Cola, Perrier, and many others.

In whatever country he finds himself, Fischer finds his little "people" are right there to cheer him on in any of the languages he knows, including French, Spanish, and German. And when he's traveling, those inked-on pen pals are very comforting on airplane trips! Fischer has put his petite people on posters in France, in magazines here and there, and on greeting cards, where they're as happy to cheer up others as they are their "boss."

Ron Morgan

Ron Morgan, who has been with the FAA in various capacities for twenty-eight years, started his career in aviation as an air traffic controller in Los Angeles and reached the full-performance level in a supervisory and managerial capacity. "I'm one of those people who started from the bottom," he says. Morgan also holds a commercial pilot's license but doesn't have a lot of time for piloting these days. As the FAA's director of air traffic, he is responsible for 575 air traffic control facilities and roughly 24,000 air traffic control professionals, from Guam to the domestic U.S. to the Caribbean, with some representatives in Europe. There are 254 people in the Washington headquarters alone. What that means is a schedule so busy that he had to arrange to do our phone interview from Anchorage, Alaska, at 6 A.M. his time. Nevertheless, Morgan declares, "It's a wonderful job."

Steve Symonds

Steve Symonds, who first started teaching Fearless Flyers groups in 1979, knows a thing or two about stormy weather. He has been with the Australian Bureau of Meteorology since 1969, starting as a weather observer in Australia's steamy Northern Territory and in Antarctica. He has worked as a technical officer and senior technical officer at several airports around Australia, including Mascot and Bankstown in the Sydney area, and in 1987, he became the public relations officer in the Bureau of Meteorology's New South Wales Regional Office in Sydney.

Lyn Williams

Lyn Williams was so keen to pursue his boyhood desire to fly planes that he abandoned his study of dentistry at the University of Sydney to drive trucks for an ice cream company to pay for his flight training. In January of 1967, at the age of nineteen, Williams received a cadet pilot scholarship from Qantas. He earned his commercial license and instrument rating in September 1968.

After two years in the Australian Army Aviation Corps, Williams taught flying at the Royal Aero Club of New South Wales before joining Qantas to fly Boeing 707s in mid-1972. Two years later, he was endorsed as a second officer on the 747. Among his aviation achievements was crewing on a flight to Darwin in Australia's Northern Territory on Dec. 26, 1974, when a record number of 694 passengers and crew were evacuated because of Cyclone Tracey. Fifty people were killed by the storm on the ground, and Darwin was almost totally destroyed.

Promoted to first officer and then to captain, Williams became certified to fly the 747-400 in 1989 and regularly flies all of Qantas's routes serviced by that enormous aircraft, including to and from the United Kingdom and Europe, Africa, Asia, New Zealand, and the United States. He is married to Marie Williams, the retired Qantas senior flight attendant interviewed in this book, and they live in Kangaroo Point, a suburb south of the Sydney airport.

Marie Williams

Marie Williams started her career at Qantas in May 1973 and was a "flight hostess," as they were called in those days, working for nine years on 707s, 767s, and 747s. In August 1982, she became a training flight hostess, evaluating flight hostesses on their operational skills on board the aircraft. She explains that the only promotional opportunities at that time were to the position of senior flight hostess or training flight hostess, until 1983, when women became "flight attendants" equal with men for promotions. That year, Williams was promoted to the position of senior flight attendant. In 1989, she completed the chief flight attendant training course and held that position until 1991. She is married to Lyn Williams, the Qantas captain interviewed in this book.

My thanks also to the following people:

- Kirsty Melville and Chelsea Vaughn, publisher and editor, respectively, at Ten Speed Press
- Barbara King, proofreader, of Redwood City, California
- Linda Sweet, Alan Dukes's wife, who coordinated communications during the shaping of the chapter on air traffic control
- Qantas captain Lyn Williams, whose swift actions helped out enormously
- Sally Walton, a Qantas flight attendant who also works as part of the airline's service development group, who contributed the spot-quiz questions in the chapter on attendants.
- Fran Grant of the Fear of Flying Clinic in San Mateo, California
- Julian Green and Des Sullivan at Qantas Public Affairs
- Ron Morgan, Patrice Allen-Gifford, Kathryn Creedy, Bill Shumann, and Kathy Higgins at the Federal Aviation Administration in Washington, D.C.
- Ken Dejarlais at the Boeing Company in Renton, Washington
- Judy Lotas, Peter McGee, Judy Fayard, and Brian Kinahan, my fearfully flying friends
- Lisa Hauptner and Tom Bunn of SOAR, Westport, Connecticut
- Dr. Al Forgione of the Institute for Psychology of Air Travel, Boston, Massachusetts

About the Author

Debbie Seaman is a freelance journalist and recovered fearful flier who has written features for publications including the *New York Times*, *People*, the *Los Angeles Times*, *Town & Country*, and Advertising Age's *Creativity* magazine. A native of Oyster Bay, New York, and a 1975 graduate of Vassar College, Debbie worked many years in New York City for *Adweek* before working as a freelancer in Paris and then Sydney, where she contributed to *Who*, *People*'s Australian sister publication, as well as business and travel publications. She first wrote about her experience with Fearless Flyers in an article published November 24, 1996, in the *New York Times* Travel Section entitled, "Learning to Beat a Fear of Flying." She currently lives in New Canaan, Connecticut, with her Australian husband, Warren Lancaster, and their twin sons, Cameron and Lachlan.

About Qantas

Qantas, which stands for Queensland and Northern Territory Aerial Services, was formally established by Paul McGuiness and Hudson Fysh, two World War I Australian Flying Corps officers, and rancher Fergus McMaster on November 16, 1920, to fly passengers to remote rural areas of northern Australia. The airline started off with two small biplanes and operated joyrides, demonstration flights, and taxi services as a prelude to regular airmail and passenger flights.

Qantas's first scheduled flight took off on November 2, 1922, and the Charleville-Longreach-Winton-McKinlay-Cloncurry route in rural Queensland formed the genesis of the fledging airline's ambition to create an air service to England out of Darwin, Northern Territory. By 1934, in partnership with Imperial Airways (which became British Overseas Airways Corporation [BOAC], then British Airways), it flew what was called the "Empire Route," from Brisbane to Darwin, the capitals of Queensland and Northern Territory, respectively, then through what is now Indonesia to Singapore, and on through Asia to the United Kingdom. The service carried only mail initially, but the first Qantas overseas passenger flight traveled from Brisbane to Singapore in 1935.

Qantas expanded rapidly in 1947, when the Australian government purchased the shares held by BOAC as well as all remaining
shares. On December 1 of that year, Qantas inaugurated its celebrated
"Kangaroo Route," making its first independent Sydney-London flight
in a long-range Lockheed Constellation aircraft, named the *Charles
Kingford Smith*. Commercial services to Hong Kong began in 1949,
Japan in 1950, South Africa in 1952, and San Francisco and Vancouver
in 1953.

In 1998, between its core jet fleet and its aircraft operated by
regional subsidiaries, Qantas has about 150 aircraft, ranging from small
planes such as the De Havilland Dash-8 for short hops to the enormous
Boeing 747-400 for long hauls. It flies to 105 destinations in 30 countries—55 within Australia—and some of its major international ports
include London, Los Angeles, Rome, Tokyo, Johannesburg, and
Bangkok. Qantas, the oldest airline in the English-speaking world, also
holds one of the best safety records of any airline worldwide.

INDEX